Holocaust Representation

Holocaust Representation

Art within the Limits of History and Ethics

BEREL LANG

The Johns Hopkins University Press
BALTIMORE AND LONDON

9 8 7 6 5 4 3 2 1

The Johns Hopkins University Press

2715 North Charles Street

Baltimore, Maryland 21218-4363

www.press.jhu.edu

Library of Congress Cataloging-in-Publication Data will be found
at the end of this book.

A catalog record for this book is available from the British Library.

ISBN 0-8018-6415-1

For Delby, Michaela, and for the three sisters and their families:
Elka and Avraham, Chaya and Mordechai, Chana and David—
in affectionate and grateful remembrance

The land they lived shaped the landscape of memory

Contents

Preface and Acknowledgments

Anyone who recognizes that the Holocaust poses unusual problems of representation also, in my view, admits the possibility of limits that apply to or constrain such representation. In two earlier works—an edited volume (*Writing and the Holocaust*, 1988) and a monograph (*Act and Idea in the Nazi Genocide*, 1990)—and now, as the connective theme among the essays gathered here, I have considered the implications of this possibility, also proposing, as a further step, to demonstrate how certain limits based on a combination of historical and ethical constraints impinge on representations or images of the Holocaust, as a matter of both fact and right.

The prima facie evidence that such conditions or limits do apply seems to me apparent in the recurring controversies about specific Holocaust images. Those controversies range from disputes about the authenticity of the experience "imaged" (as in recent disagreements over the truth status of Benjamin Wilkomirski's "memoir," *Fragments*) to conflicts about permissible modes of representation (in objections to the "comic" motif of the Benigni film *Life Is Beautiful*) to the broadest arguments, which question *any* aestheticizing of the Holocaust and whose originary point remains Theodor Adorno's charge of "barbarism" against poetry after Auschwitz. Sharp as the disagreements between opposing views on these issues have been, it seems to me still more significant that even in conflict they assume as a common premise that the problem of Holocaust representation—what can or should be represented of that event, and how—is both real and important, warranting attention to an extent commanded by few other contemporary or past historical events, and with implications as well for the concept of representation more generally.

The attempts I have made to follow this premise beyond its starting point have turned out, however, to be unexpectedly (for me) contentious. For although almost nobody who has reflected on the matter would deny the extraordinary character of the Holocaust as a historical and moral "event" or the unusual demands it would be likely to make on whatever was imagined to describe it, the possibility that its extraordinary character might entail restrictions or limits or even exclusions in the means of its representation has been regarded by some commentators as an attack on the individual disciplines or arts with which they identify themselves, principally literature and the visual arts but also, to a lesser extent, historiography itself.

This reaction to the prospect of limits has at times been heated and even acrimonious, and although whatever substantive objections figure in it must of course be met on their own terms, the disproportion between heat and light in the reaction seems to me to reflect the compartmentalized environment of the academy—from which, evidently, not even the study of an event like the Holocaust is immune—rather than the issue itself or even my formulation of it. For that issue, whatever judgment one finally makes of it, is, with all its complexities and difficulties, quite straightforward in its terms. Indeed what is asserted here is hardly more than the modest claim, also denied by virtually nobody, that the character of a subject or topic will, and should, have some direct bearing on the form of its expression. Whether and to what extent this commonplace applies to Holocaust images is, of course, a question, but one that is no more beyond discussion that may conclude by ruling some ideals or practices in or out than is any other instance of moral or aesthetic or historiographic analysis.

To be sure, I have also attempted to show that such limits have a special force where Holocaust images are concerned; indeed, that the pressure exerted by those limits has often been evident in the representations themselves and that it has also been responsible for certain of the innovations (through the "blurred genres") that Holocaust writing has fostered as well as for certain noticeable emphases (as in the trope of realism or verisimilitude). About the evidence for this claim, as well as on the question of what conclusions follow from it, obviously there can be reasonable disagreement. Some accounts have concluded that what is involved here is nothing more than the normal life or history of the process of representation, and I would agree with this conclusion, but with a substantial qualification: that the "normal" life of representation always includes acknowledgment of historical and moral factors that do, or at least should, affect the shaping of the images of representation. It is in this claim, it seems to me, that the core of disputes about Holocaust images is to be found, and I would hope that the essays collected here, apart from the question of whether their specific conclusions are persuasive, will at least win acknowledgment of the significance of the problem to which they are directed. Again, the question of what Holocaust images are capable of or justified in doing seems to me both real and urgent, and indeed the purview and implications of that question, are much broader than the representation of that one event. Indeed their origins, as the title of this volume is meant to suggest, evoke the conception of "images," which have been the subject of debate (and limitations) since the earliest days of both philosophy and religion in the West.

In Part I of this volume I face directly the problem of Holocaust representation, beginning with what seems to me the prima facie evidence of the combined historical and moral pressures that the creators of Holocaust images have recognized and reacted to. Evidence of this appears, for example, in the "blurred genres" of Holocaust writing (Chapter 2)—the attempts to challenge the conventions of genre, partly in order to emphasize the *unconventional* character of their subject but also, and more substantively, to find a means adequate for representing the specific features of the Nazi genocide, which stretch or breach the standard norms of representation. Other prima facie evidence of the unusual pressure on Holocaust images appears in the recurrent appeal to an ideal of historical authenticity even in openly "imaginative" works that have the Holocaust as their subject (Chapter 1). What this evidence points to, in my view, is the constraints on Holocaust representation clearly exemplified in differences between "imaginative" and historical discourses that have the Holocaust as their subject (Chapter 3); if historical writing cannot sustain the alleged distinction between fact and value, then the assumption of that distinction in imaginative writing would also fail. In Chapter 4, I turn to the fiction/nonfiction distinction, asking whether that distinction itself is fictional or non-fictional—and finding from three case studies in Holocaust writing evidence for the distinction's moral, rather than cognitive or aesthetic, basis. The boundary concept that tests all of these proposals is the possibility of Holocaust *mis*representation (Chapter 5), which itself pre-supposes the ethical and historical constraints discussed in the earlier chapters. The denial of that possibility, with the severe consequences that would follow (including the possibility of Holocaust denial), is not only invited but entailed by the rejection in principle of all constraints on representation.

Part II views the subject of Holocaust images more obliquely and from a variety of angles, reflecting on the work of individual historians and artists (Chapter 6), inquiring about the possible national differences in "reader response" to writings about the Holocaust (Chapter 7), and considering the challenge that postmodernist analysis might or ought to make to "thinking the Holocaust" (Chapter 8). It will be evident that in my view, just as the Holocaust itself is to be understood in standard historical and moral categories (even when we judge that these have been breached), so the "rupture" that postmodernism finds in the Holocaust undermines rather than strengthens the force of its representations. This theme appears again, in a more generalized form, in Chapter 9, "Art Worship and Its Images."

IN THINKING and writing about these issues, I have benefited from discussions, in conversation or correspondence, with a number of friends or with strangers who through these discussions became friends. Not that there was or would be agreement among us even on the central issues involved in these topics but that we assumed as a common premise that the subject addressed was more important than any disagreements that might arise in our understanding of it, more important, indeed, than anything we could say about it. This meant that what we held in common continued to matter more than anything that divided us—a sense of solidarity that was all the more heartening because of the harshly isolating subject of the Holocaust itself. The study of that event could not, after all, be unmarked by its features. And so, for this fellowship, and more specifically for the conversations, letters, readings, responses, reviews, *words:* my thanks to Ernst van Alphen, Aharon Appelfeld, Hedva Ben-Israel, Michael Andre Bernstein, Joyce Brodsky, Brian Cheyette, Saul Friedländer, Geoffrey Hartman, Sara Horowitz, Lawrence Langer, Andrew Leak, Herbert Lindenberger, Leslie Morris, Bert Nepaulsingh, Cynthia Ozick, George Paizis, Vera Schwarcz, Richard Stamelman, Hayden White, and James Young. I remember here as well my late teacher Albert Hofstadter, who joined to the concept of an "aesthetic education" a constant and acute emphasis on its ethical presuppositions. Neither he nor the others mentioned are responsible, of course, for what I have made of their efforts—although I know they would understand how I have come to say even what they might object to.

My wife, Helen S. Lang, has been certainly tried and constantly true as a reader; her support for this as always has been integral to the work. Our daughters, Ariella Lang and Jessica Lang, first as an audience and increasingly in their own thinking, have begun to address certain of the questions raised here, and that interest has provided me with an additional incentive.

Earlier versions of a number of the essays in this book have appeared in journals or books, and I am grateful to the publishers for their permission to make use of those essays as a starting point for the revised versions that appear here. These include "Writing-the-Holocaust: Toward the Condition of History," in A. Leak and G. Paizis, eds., *The Holocaust and Literature: Real Fictions* (London, 1998); "Representation within the Limits," in S. Friedländer, ed., *Probing the Limits of Representation* (Cambridge, 1992; copyright © by The President and

Fellows of Harvard College); "The Importance of Holocaust-*Mis*representation," in *History and Theory,* 1995; "Hilberg on Hilberg: The Man and the Book," in *Judaism,* 1997; "Translating the Holocaust: For Whom Does One Write?" (in Hebrew), introduction to Berel Lang, *Act and Idea in the Nazi Genocide* (Jerusalem, 2000); and "Art-Worship," in *Michigan Quarterly Review,* 1999.

Holocaust Representation

Introduction

Art within the Limits

The phrase "art within the limits" would be a provocation even if the limits were left unspecified. Much more than science, which at once acknowledges its own continuing obsolescence and promises a full and final accounting of the world of nature, art has appeared in the drive of modernism (still more forcefully in postmodernism) as creation unfettered: engaged in the construction of original worlds (and by implication, of selves) whose attraction originates precisely there, in the fact that they create their own laws or limits, with the possibility never far off of superseding these laws or limits through others. In large measure because of the lure of this possibility, the quarrel between art and ethics—the *suspicion* of art—inscribed by Plato in his ideal Republic has ever since been a constant presence in Western thought, one of that small number of themes that have persisted both in a significant intellectual tradition (rationalism) and in a variety of more general and popular expressions, mainly in the principal religious traditions.

This quarrel has been far from one-sided, although the issues at stake are so close to the center of cultural commitment and practice that at times one side has overwhelmed the other to a degree that seems to have settled the matter once and for all—only to find soon afterward, of course, that this was not the case at all. At other times a more even opposition has produced a balance between the two camps, which, as if in resentment of that balance, have then contrived to talk past rather than to each other even in the rare encounters between them. The view according to which art transcends the more ordinary expressive forms of ethics—the at once more regular and more easily regulated forms—has had the undoubted power of art and the artist to argue from as a basis; the quarrel could not have been as persistent and pointed as it has been without this. Thus the celebration of art in the Renaissance and in nineteenth-century romanticism, at once in theory and in practice, has been joined by a tradition of religious art in arguing for the importance of art as expressing a human impulse or need that was no less fundamental (and in certain ways even more so) than any others among those held to constitute the vague but unavoidable concept of human nature that, in the many different versions given it, nonetheless recurs as a concept in all cultural and moral analysis.

It may seem late in the day to call attention to this quarrel, especially at a time when tolerance as both a public and a private virtue is professed by most of the reigning ideologies, whatever else they disagree about. And indeed the terms of the quarrel in contemporary thought and practice usually are not formulated as the "either-or" of Plato, for whom the philosophical stakes were supreme, but as a more nuanced critique in which art is questioned ethically not as a whole but in its parts, that is, in respect only to certain of its constructs and appearances. Admittedly, even this more qualified treatment is not without its opponents on either side: from the perspective still of "art for art's sake," which sanctions in art the limitless reach of the creative imagination, and so also accords to the artist and his work the exemption from all moral judgment that George Orwell trenchantly named, in his essay of the same title, the "benefit of clergy"; and, from the other side, on the part of a strong—in some parts of the world, growing—"fundamentalist" impulse for which the antinomianism of art would make it suspect even if the hostility to art were not also joined, as it obviously is, to the immediacy of art's pleasures.

This quarrel between extremes cannot simply be written off as excess or indulgence, although something of those failings undoubtedly figures in them both. The status of art finally extends both to metaphysical and ontological grounds and to the analysis of human nature within that more general framework; at least this far—that is, in formal terms—Plato's analysis remains as a paradigm quite apart from any judgment on his specific views. For anyone who takes art and ethics seriously in their own respective terms, the question of whether or how they are related to each other, how they affect or impinge on each other, cannot be avoided. And insofar as the question of the nature of truth also cannot be avoided in considering aesthetic or ethical judgment, whether through the conclusion that it bears on them only in a limited sense or even by its irrelevance to them, the classic Platonic triad of the good, the true, and the beautiful continues to exert pressure long after its original formulation is supposed to have become obsolete.

The issues I address in the essays that make up this volume are not, however, set at this general level, even if the position proposed has implications for, and from, that level. What concerns me here in philosophical terms is a question *internal* to the institution of art, namely, what difference to the shaping of art's works the ethical and cognitive (in the context here, the historical) presence can or should make, or more concisely, what the moral and historical responsibility of art is. The institution of art is thus assumed as a given, with my question then asking about the historical and ethical constitution and limitations of that "given."

As the philosophical issue so defined is set within the bounds of art, so the occasion for raising it is also specific. The event that has come to be known as "The Holocaust" has been identified in moral terms no less emphatically than in historical terms. For the "post-Holocaust" period we now inhabit, fifty-five years after the Holocaust itself ended, the Nazi genocide against the Jews is in both these sets of terms also a given, beyond reasonable doubt: the combination of moral enormity and historical causality embodied in Heinrich Himmler's statement of purpose that "this people should disappear from the earth." What remains in dispute, however, what in fact becomes an increasingly pressing concern as the passage of time provides space for additional reflection and innovation, is the question of how such an event, *that* one in particular, can or should be "represented," what forms its "images" can or ought to take, most specifically in the forms of art that epitomize the process of representation or imaging but also in the less dramatic discourses, for example, in history or the other social sciences.

The latter question may seem to raise two radically different issues, that is, how the Holocaust can be represented and how it ought to be. This presumptive "is-ought" distinction is itself open to dispute, however, and my reason for including both sides here is not the prudential one of wishing to cover both bases; quite apart from rejecting the more general distinction—a separate matter from that addressed here—I view the two sides as interrelated in the specific cases and analyses considered here in respect to Holocaust images. It is obvious that in some sense any form of art or other representation can be imposed on any material or content. The fitting might be forced or abusive and the results parodic or disfiguring, but it can be done for virtually any imaginable case—and the images or representations thus created here would be "as you like it"; there would be no more, or more special, problems about Holocaust representation than about any other. And yet the historical evidence is clear, in the history of representation in general and for the arts more specifically, that the "genres" that have been individuated within the general space of representation have assumed characteristic roles and conventions, responding to certain subjects and not to others, seeking certain effects but making no effort in other directions: sonnets speak of love or death but not of pratfalls; sonatas do not "do" what concerti do, and the import of still-life paintings is not that of portraits, especially self-portraits. Are these patterns accidental? As has already been conceded, nobody doubts that various genres *can* be conflated, and there is no way of proving beforehand that these joinings could not be salutary, "artful." But the weight of evidence from such experiments in the past—deliberate experiments or, more often, the accidental ones of artists at work beyond their depth—argue to the contrary, insisting once again that those two elusive but persistent variables, the form and the content, however one defines them individually or together, yet matter to each other, affect the relationship between them and thus the whole that they constitute.

What do such understated and banal abstractions have to do with images and representations of the Holocaust, which neither in itself nor in the problems of its representation appears as understated or banal? A great deal, it seems to me. Because if there is characteristically a significant relation between the subject or occasion of representation (in or outside the art world) and the form by which it is expressed, then it would follow that the identifying features of the Holocaust—what makes it distinctive historically and morally—would, and should, also make a difference in the modes of its representation. What the event was, in other words, would also limit or even close out certain possibilities to the artist while opening the way to others. It might even follow, taking the premises here to an extreme and thinking also of ever larger genres of representation—so also, for example, the *genre* of art— that entire genres would be found wanting or perhaps ruled out where certain subjects or contents were concerned. The historical and ethical distinctiveness of the Holocaust evokes all of these possibilities, including the most extreme of them.

The statements thus presented are in the subjunctive mood, making assertions about possible worlds and what might be, or even what should be, *if*. . . . Can nothing be said in the present indicative? Well, in the essays that follow I attempt to do just that, to state and to face the problems of Holocaust images in terms that are unmistakable (which doesn't mean, of course, that what they assert may not be mistaken) and, more importantly, unavoidable. Since Theodor Adorno's bombshell—his proclamation that writing "lyric poetry after Auschwitz would be barbarous"—the battle has been joined, although always among uneasy allies and between opponents who often talk past rather than to or even against each other. Adorno himself would subsequently modify if not retract his verdict, but others would go even farther than he had gone. Claims that the Holocaust was "indescribable" or "ineffable" have been common; often such claims are themselves figures of speech—hyperbole, metaphor—underscoring moral and historical enormity that is not at all immune, however, to description or analysis or to the artistic imagination. And certainly images have been cast of the Holocaust that might make even those who were hostile in principle to Adorno's warning recall it wistfully in practice.

No less certainly there would be—has been—disagreement about which Holocaust images in particular "deform" or debase or diminish that event. Almost everybody, however, can name some examples of Holocaust representation that seem to them to warrant such criticism—and it seems to me that this finding is itself strong evidence, more than only prima facie, of the limits posited around the representations of this event. This event, in contrast to so many others for which the question of "boundaries" in their representation reduces quite simply to the question of whether what is viewed is interesting or original. That such limits are often vague or unarticulated is less to the point than that they are appealed to and applied: it is the assumption of their relevance that is decisive. To be sure, debates concerning the circulation of pornography recur periodically; the representation of violence has recently drawn attention; and even charges of religious sacrilege directed against literary or photographic images have been heard—and not only from Iran. But the "cause" recently evoking the most numerous and the most heated disagreements has been the Holocaust and its "images": in films like Roberto Benigni's quasi-comic *Life Is Beautiful,* in the intense controversy over Benjamin Wilkomirski's *Fragments,* which viewed on one level is nothing more than a controversy over whether that book should be classified as nonfiction or fiction, in the recurring disputes about what a Holocaust memorial should look like. Obviously there is more at stake in these quarrels than whether Benigni's film deserved an Academy Award or where Wilkomirski's book should be shelved in libraries or bookstores of whether Berlin should be the site of a Holocaust memorial at all. What comes to the fore here is driven by the convergence of ethical and historical questions—how "true" Benigni's film is to life (and death) in the concentration camps, whether the events recounted by Wilkomirski "actually" occurred, whose viewpoint a memorial can or ought to represent. It might be asked why these or other such questions matter. Indeed, some responses have insisted that they do not. But many of the reactions assume, albeit without saying exactly how or why, that they matter a great deal, a claim that is inexplicable except as based on the combination of moral and historical criteria that the essays of this volume discuss and that will lead there to the formulation of certain limits that in my view apply to Holocaust images.

Two types of objections have been raised against the view of Holocaust representation that I have been sketching. The first is an instrumental or practical objection: that on the premise that awareness about the Holocaust is important and a desirable goal of public education (whether formal or informal), and given the diverse tastes and capacities of groups and individuals and the variety of possible representations or images, there is really nothing more to be said, certainly nothing to be criticized, no limits to be set or even hoped for in Holocaust representation—in general or, except perhaps in extreme cases like concentration camp pornography, in particular. Art—low at least as often and effectively as high—is capable of reaching audiences that other means of expression cannot. And to claim that certain Holocaust images or means of representation are more fitting or more in accord than others with the historical complexity or moral enormity of the Holocaust is only a dictate that imposes one person's (or group's) taste or judgment on others—high-handed at best, morally dubious at worst.

It would be foolish to deny the force of the argument from numbers that stands behind this objection, and nothing I say in the essays collected here does this. Nor do I argue against the position that the more widespread the awareness of the event of the Holocaust, by almost any representational means, the better; indeed, in Chapter 2 I present a defense, admittedly a limited one, of this view. But as an argument in behalf of Holocaust images as such, these claims beg one crucial question and avoid a second one altogether. The question-begging claim is this: that "awareness" of the Holocaust is an overriding value, one that holds quite apart from the means or the medium used. And the objection to this is clear and obvious. Does the context (and content) that produces awareness make no difference to the subject? Any such claim would justify a range of educational means extending to physical coercion or bribery as well as to any idiom or form of representation in more conventional "texts."

To be sure, it is not only the "practical" argument in favor of Holocaust images that begs the question of the "consequences" of art: it is a longstanding scandal of the traditions of art and aesthetics together that so little attention has been given and so little evidence gathered on exactly what those consequences are. In several of the essays brought together here and in my earlier book *Act and Idea in the Nazi Genocide* I present my own rendering of that question, but the point at the moment is not whether my view is convincing in its claim that the intrinsic personalization and naturalizing effect of art stands to *mis*represent or distort, and so to diminish and violate, certain subjects, the Holocaust among them. The general principle at stake is that to hold up awareness or "consciousness" of a particular subject as intrinsically valuable without addressing the context in which that consciousness occurs and the consequences that may follow from it is to do nothing beyond noticing or comparing the box-office "take."

The question entirely avoided in this first objection is a compound one of character and quality. If the criterion for justifying Holocaust images is accessibility, or more positively, "attraction"—for example, the allure of art—then the sole means of drawing distinctions is numerical. The film *Schindler's List* drew audiences in the tens of millions; Claude Lanzmann's eight-hour-long *Shoah* is unlikely ever to reach more than a small fraction of that audience. Thus, in terms of comparative value or quality based on numbers or "appeal," the conclusion to be drawn is uncontestable; it is a conclusion, however, rarely defended by those who object to the alternative criteria compressed into the few terms mentioned above but one that would then point a significant question: Which of the two films "represents" more authentically or more deeply or more fully the event of the Holocaust itself? To apply to Holocaust images the nostrum that in matters of taste *non disputandum est* is viewed as excessive even by those for whom a version of the utilitarian calculus is the basis of evaluation. But if that is the case, then two alternatives remain as the basis of all judgment or comparison: the appeal to numbers (a new application of the calculus) and the proposal of another, more substantive means—one that in the view presented here involves historical and ethical criteria.

The second objection to the position that emerges in this volume comes in two parts, or more accurately, in two versions. The first is that the general view of art on which I base the cautionary notes registered about Holocaust images is, quite simply, mistaken. Without at all denying that abuses of the artistic media can occur, even that there can be "bad" art, this objection to what I warn against is no more than a possibility open to any kind of activity—and thus not at all specific to artistic representation, still less to representations of the Holocaust in particular. Artistic representation (according to this view) is in fact capable of conveying truth or knowledge—moral knowledge or even knowledge in its more conventional, epistemic sense—no less certainly, and in some instances even more so, than other expressive means. In other words, if it is the dignity or integrity of truth that is an issue, Holocaust images may convey those qualities every bit as surely and (this reintroduces the first objection noted above) even more accessibly than other expressive or representational means.

This objection moves the disagreement to the level of ontology and metaphysics, considering the "objects" of art in relation to the other kinds of objects, the "knowledge" or "truth" conveyed by art as that compares with the knowledge or truth conveyed by other means. Even to confront the issue of Holocaust images on that level would, in my view, already be a concession to the arguments I have presented. It would imply recognition of the fallibility of art, conceding that as a means of representation, art is indeed contingent, not necessary, and thus that it is subject to the same scrutiny and judgment in terms of criteria of truth and ethics to which other forms of discourse are subject. And more than this: I do not say that the pitfalls to which art in general and Holocaust representation in particular is subject *ensure* its failure, that they are intrinsic or necessary flaws. There are Holocaust images in virtually all the arts—fiction, poetry, painting, architecture— that have amply demonstrated this (to the degree that aesthetic judgment can be said to be demonstrated at all). But the point that stands out for me in such work is that it reflects—in this one respect, more than other acclaimed representations—an unusual inventiveness and power of imagination insofar as it has overcome the characteristic features of art that stand as liabilities in respect to the subject of the Holocaust.

It seems to me that the central question to ask in the analysis of Holocaust representation is just how the deepest and most urgent Holocaust art, in the person of such figures as Paul Celan or Aharon Appelfeld, or visual artists like Samuel Baks or Shimon Attie, has succeeded in turning an oppositional impulse into its own strength. It is not always the case that artistic achievement is linked to innovation in the forms or genres of art; it has been argued in fact that the largest achievements in modes of representation have typically occurred within established genres and aesthetic conventions since these provide a fulcrum for the artist to move from. But in the case of Holocaust images this has quite plainly *not* been the case, and the reason for this also seems clear: the pressures exerted by their common subject are such that the associations of the traditional forms—the developmental order of the novel, the predictability of prosody, the comforting representations of landscape or portrait in painting—are quite inadequate for the images of a subject with the moral dimensions and impersonal will of the Holocaust. Thus the constant turning in Holocaust images to *difference:* to the use of silence as means and metaphor, to obliqueness in representation that approaches the abstraction of abstract painting without yet conceding its goals, to the uses of allegory and fable and surrealism, to the blurring of traditional genres not just for the sake of undoing them but in the interests of combining certain of their elements that otherwise had been held apart.

As mentioned before, conventional art forms have certainly been strong and popular influences with audiences in search of Holocaust images. But again, the question of whether the statistics demonstrating this prove anything significant about the value of such representation or about its effects remains open. It remains a not very well concealed secret that little is known about the effects of representations or images of any sort, about any subject, on their audiences, and if this is not in itself an argument against Holocaust images, it is certainly an argument against justifying all and any of them simply because of the subject on which they are based. Certainly it leaves the issue I would press—of judging and discriminating among Holocaust images in terms of their aesthetic, historical, and moral qualities—quite open, open enough to search for and apply other, independent grounds for such discrimination and judgment.

The second version of this (second) objection to the position I defend, which privileges historical over aesthetic discourse, argues the converse: where the first version claims that I underestimate the characteristic power of art, the second argues that I overestimate—or even more emphatically, mistake—the power or character of historical discourse. For if, in a simplified rendering, I present the dangers surrounding Holocaust images as originating in the figurative—and so personalized, individualized, *humanized*—effect of art and the artist, then I appear to be blind to that presence in historical discourse and its images, which are, after all, also figurative, subjective, and finally tendentious. I engage this objection quite directly in Chapter 4, and so I address it only summarily here: if there is no crucial difference between imaginative and historical writing, then there can be no crucial difference between denials that the Holocaust occurred and the discourse that affirms its occurrence, and no difference between either of these and the broad range of fictional and poetic images of the Holocaust that began to appear within the Holocaust itself and have continued to appear since.

The contrary position is clear: there is indeed a crucial difference between these representations, and the difference on the part of historical or documentary discourse that has passed the test of verification amounts to a moral difference as well. If ever facts have spoken for themselves, this is the case for the body of fact surrounding the Holocaust. It is not that images or the act of imagination are irrelevant to this body but that their primary commission or role remains to conceive of, to imagine, the *possibility* of the Holocaust. To be sure, that sense of possibility is grounded in the actuality of that event (itself an argument for the primacy, at least in logical sequence, of historical representation). But the sense of possibility as the imagination works at it is by its nature a challenge to limits, even to their possibility. There are undoubtedly many directions to which reflection or memory or the imagination may turn in the aftermath of the Holocaust, but the one direction on which any such movement is dependent is in knowing and following the contours of what that event was, as it was and how it came to be. And that dependence, which on the face of it is both logical and chronological, in my view also attests to a moral order.

Undoubtedly, in the irony of dialectical thinking, a condition of Holocaust representation is the possibility of Holocaust *mis*representation—as a condition of Holocaust images is the possibility of their defacement, and a condition of Holocaust history the possibility of its denial. But surely the only defense against the second of each of these pairs is what the elements of history itself disclose even after allowing for its narrative structures, ideological turns, and high or low motives. Is it indeed possible to neutralize these factors? There are two ways to answer this question. The first is to consider what the consequences would be if it were *not* possible. No matter how fearsome the consequences, this would not answer or settle the question, but to consider the possibility that Holocaust denial is only another (and incommensurable) narrative of the history of the Third Reich must be a sobering prolegomenon to any future representation. The second way is at once more hopeful and more substantive since it points to the fact of facts. I claim by this that there are indeed *extra*narrative, *extra*ideological, *extra*contextual grounds that diverse, even conflicting narratives, ideologies, and contexts must in common confront. Nobody doubts that certain predictions about chemical or physical behavior are more accurate than others, and that there are good reasons for this. History is not chemistry or physics (although it might be argued that they are rather subdivisions of history), but the matter from which it sets out is not different in principle from the matter from which they set out.

It might be objected that even if everything said so far in these opening pages were assumed to be true for the sake of argument, it would not follow that historical representation, with the ethical dimension then associated with it, should be privileged over other forms of representation in respect to events like the Holocaust, for which the question of ethical significance is crucial. Even if all other forms of representation were logically or systematically dependent on a historical substructure or subtext, this would not mean that what was built on that foundation could not realize certain ends that the foundation by itself had not envisaged. But I do not deny this as a possibility nor indeed as fact. Clearly, many representations in diverse genres and metagenres have gone far beyond the elementary data of the "chronicle" or documentary record. These representations would, in my account, be at the center, the point-zero, of Holocaust images, constituting in effect a nonrepresentational representation. And it is clear that some of those works, in fiction and poetry as well as in the abstractions of reflection, have contributed significantly to both the understanding and the representation of the Holocaust. There is little point in naming names here—although I do this to some extent in the essays that follow—since the disagreements that the process invites shift the issue away from the central one of whether there *are* important differences between the representations that have such qualities and those that do not. This, it seems to me, remains central to the question, the problem, the issue of Holocaust images. And since all of those images depend in their origins on the elements of history; and since all of them, once projected, depend on the continuing test of history in its conjunction with moral principle, there is a strong sense in which the chronicle of the Holocaust—the rudimentary details of the answers to the questions of who, what, and when—remains at the center and as a test of whatever else is constructed on them. Both as a matter of fact and as a matter of justice.

There are, admittedly, other ways of posing the thesis that thus emerges in the following pages. It might be asked, for example, how, or to what extent, aesthetic considerations should be encouraged or permitted to obtrude on Holocaust images. A "beautiful" Holocaust poem or painting? An "evocative" Holocaust novel or film? A Holocaust dance or symphony that is a "tour de force"? To isolate such standard and valued terms of praise is in itself to face the problem of Holocaust representation, and to come close as well to recognizing the pressures of historical and ethical limits that I have been speaking about. Nobody would argue that the "best" representation or image of the Holocaust would be to reproduce it accurately, to the last detail—that is, to recreate the Holocaust itself. The value of historical nonrepresentational representation is exactly here, in its representation of the events that occurred without mediation but also without bringing the events themselves once again to life. If knowledge and understanding of the Holocaust are the goal of all Holocaust images, then it will be here, along these lines, that we should continue to look, and to do this even—or, more accurately, especially—when the means employed move farther and farther away from that center.

There may be future representations or images that will indeed illuminate, edify, perhaps transform the viewer and all understanding of

Art within the Limits

the Holocaust. Perhaps they will do this apart from or even in opposition to the claims of historical representation. But if the past serves as a guide, the Holocaust images that have the strongest claims on their viewers will be, as they have been, closely bound to historical reference, cued on its detail and imagined within its limits. And these boundaries will be recognized not on the basis of legislation, not even from the precedents of Holocaust images that have followed along the same lines, but from the demands made on such representation by its subject. Any claim that "the facts speak for themselves" must itself expect to be questioned; but if such an antirepresentational statement ever applies, it does so in respect to the event of the Holocaust, and it does so there in respect to both the historical and the ethical limits set by that event for anyone who approaches it.

Image and Fact $\quad$ I

The Problem of Holocaust Representation

Writing the Holocaust | 1

Toward the Condition of History

It has become almost a matter of course that writings about the Holocaust should allude—often in their titles, but if not there, in the texts—to the "incomprehensibility," the "unspeakability" or "ineffability," and so, even more cumbersomely, the "unwritability," of the Holocaust as a subject. Yet in these very discourses the "incomprehensible" is explained (at least the effort is made), the "unspeakable" and the "ineffable" are pretty clearly spoken (or spoken about), and the "unwritable" is written. One might think that the incongruity of these conjunctions would by now have impressed itself sufficiently to force any such allusion to question itself. For understood literally, "speaking the unspeakable" is a straightforward contradiction—it can't be done—and even if we give the phrase an honorific gloss by calling it a paradox, we only defer the issue of how to reconcile its inconsistent elements. Maimonides concluded that in a sacred text there can be no contradictions, thus that apparent contradictions must be figurative rather than literal in meaning and so are not, strictly speaking, contradictory at all. Inconsistencies in secular texts are unlikely to bow to this same principle, but we know enough about the event at the center of the essays assembled here—an event as close to sacred, after all, as anything in a secular world is likely to be—to know that calling it unspeakable is often also, even always, figurative. In its manner of speaking, it heaps hyperbole atop metaphor, verging on that striking figure of speech, the *praeteritio,* in which a speaker announces that he will not speak about something, when what becomes immediately evident is that the purpose of this denial is to do just that, in effect to say precisely what he has declared he will not be saying.

Most commonly we meet this figure in political discourse—for example, when a candidate for office declines to violate his listeners' sensibilities by recalling his honorable friend's sordid past. For the subject addressed here, which involves true moral enormity, we hear it referred to as unspeakable, and we usually hear soon afterward a fairly detailed description of what is unspeakable, that description intended, of course, to prove that the designation was warranted. In this way, a "negative rhetoric" emerges along the more traditional side of "negative theology"—both of them so strong and definite in their respective commitments that simple affirmation is hardly commensurate with their force. Surely it is neither accidental nor inconsistent that the best-known statements that place the Holocaust beyond (and so against) representation have come from authors as dissimilar as Theodor Adorno, Elie Wiesel, and George Steiner, who, through the representations they subsequently allowed themselves, have also been among the most profound influences on the content as well as the form of Holocaust writing.

I propose at the outset of this discussion, then—and once and for all, if I could—to "de-figure" this figure of the Holocaust; to claim instead that the Holocaust is speakable, that it has been, will be (certainly here), and, most of all, ought to be spoken. Virtually all claims to the contrary—in those variations on the unspeakable that cover also the indescribable, the unthinkable, the unimaginable, the incredible—come embedded in yards of writing that attempt to overcome the inadequacy of language in representing moral enormity at the same time that they assert its presence; certainly they hope to find for their own assertions of such inadequacy a useful—*telling*—place in its shadow.

It is self-evident, at any rate, that no Holocaust writing gives preference to silence—although silence is itself, after all, a distinctive literary genre, one that Isaac Babel first named and mastered (and then fell victim to). Indeed, silence arguably remains a criterion for all discourse (Holocaust or not), a constant if phantom presence that stipulates that whatever is written ought to be justifiable as more probative, more incisive, more *revealing,* than its absence or, more cruelly, its erasure. Put differently, this criterion poses the question whether the loss of any particular text would not, in moral or cognitive terms, manifest itself as a gain—a question especially pertinent to Holocaust writing just because of the weightiness of that subject. I concede that, barring the most exceptional instances (e.g., the subgenre of Holocaust pornography), the price of silence about the Holocaust in lieu of its representation as a general principle—that cost inviting the vacuum of forgetfulness—is too high. But even this concession should not cause us to forget that the basic measure of any piece of Holocaust writing is not the possibility of alternative formulations—which may be beyond its author's ken or will—but the erasure of what he or she *has* written, that is, silence.

If we assume in any image or "representation" a construct that substitutes the representation for an original, then since no representation can ever *be* that original, representations will also never be quite adequate, however close they come to the original. This is what we might punningly call the "original sin" of representation—for which Plato, notwithstanding his caricature of it in the *Republic,* provides a ground. And even if we reject the metaphysical framework implicit in this claim of intrinsic inadequacy, it seems clear that now, more than fifty years into the post-Holocaust, the question confronting us is not whether the Holocaust is speakable but how to justify what *is* spoken. My comments here turn mainly to the latter question, although I defer consideration of how ethical premises shape, or ought to shape, Holocaust discourse in order to consider an aspect of the more neutral, descriptive topic of Holocaust genres—moving only after that to examine the relationship between those genres and the ethical imperative that underlies them.

So: Holocaust genres. The inventiveness of twentieth-century history has seen to it that one understanding of this phrase would be that Holocausts themselves may come in genres. My more ordinary interest here, however, is in the kinds of literary representation that consider or assume the Holocaust as a subject for the images or representations for which I propose to detail one common feature in particular. On the basis of that feature, I shall eventually propose to subsume the Holocaust genres that are considered as "literature"—conventional ones like the diary, the memoir, the novel, together with less conventional ones like oral histories and even the historical treatise—under a single, more inclusive rubric, concluding that Holocaust writing *as such* has the features of a genre, rooted in its moral connection to the writing of history.

That discussion is driven by one large but brief thesis, a thesis that comes, however, with a number of corollaries (and strings) attached. The thesis is that Holocaust writing characteristically "aspires constantly to the condition of history" (appropriating here a phrase in Walter Pater's reflection that "art aspires constantly to the condition of music"). More fully, my claim is that whether in representation or in fact—an ambiguity present, after all, in the very term *history,* which denotes both historical writing and the events written about—Holocaust genres are bound (anchored) historically, in part because they set out from a particular historical point but more importantly because historical authenticity is also what they in common purport to realize. For Holocaust genres, in other words, history functions both as an occasion—that is, as a subject and incentive—and also as an end, one that affects not only the standard features of those genres but even their most artful or inventive elements, with the reason for this constancy to be found in an underlying ethical ground.

This broad and amorphous claim requires elaboration on all its sides. But a structure for the outline of its basic terms can be seen in a division among three categories, or "orders," of Holocaust writing that serve as evidence for the thesis and are, I believe, intelligible only in light of it. The first of these is the large group of Holocaust writings that at once claim historical veracity (openly or by implication) and assert or indicate their differences from historical writing as such; the second is a smaller but substantial group of Holocaust writings that presuppose (but without claiming) historical veracity and disclose that presupposition in their subtexts or contexts; the third is the group of

Holocaust writings that explicitly present themselves as historiographic, ascribing to themselves the status of something like Ranke's ideal of writing history as it "actually [*eigentlich*] was."

The first of these groups includes the large body of Holocaust writings that profess historicity, the exemplary genre here being the diary, but encompassing also other, more mediated forms like the memoir, the autobiography, the "oral history," the nonfictional fiction (in novels or short stories), all of which evoke and then rely on the reader's belief in their verisimilitude. I refer to the diary as exemplary among these —the Ringelblum or Czerniakow diaries from the Warsaw Ghetto, the (collective) chronicle of the Lodz Ghetto (1941–44), the Klemperer diary from Dresden[1]—inasmuch as the diary includes two elements typical not of historical narrative but of the movement of history itself.

The first of these two elements appears in the direct representation (an enactment) of the contingency of historical time—insofar as the diarist writes in ignorance of what the next moment, let alone any longer period, holds for the events he describes or, more pointedly, for himself. Thus open and unknown, the future is also incapable of retroactively shaping the events or reactions (or predictions) noted in the diary. Of course, Ringelblum (for example) had few illusions, even early on, about what was in store for either the Warsaw Ghetto or himself. But there is nonetheless a crucial difference between that anticipation as it entered his diary and the writing in even the least self-indulgent memoirs, such as those of Primo Levi,[2] which nonetheless reach into the past from the vantage point of its outcome and, more decisively, of its author's survival. The second element, related to the first, is the exclusion from the writing of the diary of all revision, the absence of second thoughts or afterthoughts, which, were they admitted, would unavoidably taint or refigure the past (revision even for

1. Emmanuel Ringelblum, *Notes from the Warsaw Ghetto,* trans. and ed. Jacob Sloan (New York: Schocken, 1974); Adam Czerniakow, *The Warsaw Diaries of Adam Czerniakow,* ed. Raul Hilberg, Stanislaw Staron, and Josef Kermisz (New York: Stein & Day, 1979); Lucjan Dobroszycki, ed., *The Chronicle of the Lodz Ghetto, 1941–1944* (New Haven: Yale Univ. Press, 1984); Victor Klemperer, *I Will Bear Witness,* trans. Martin Chalmers (New York: Random House, 1998).

2. Primo Levi, *Survival in Auschwitz,* trans. Stuart Woolf (New York: Collier Books, 1961); idem, *The Reawakening,* trans. Stuart Woolf (New York: Summit, 1985).

"purely" historical purposes would lose that purity in the process). The diary comes as close as representation can to performing the events it cites rather than to describing them; it is an act in, if not fully of, the history it relates.

The other genres in this first category are more conventional in their representational roles: the memoir or autobiography, which depicts the past through the filter of memory, employing that filter tacitly, as Primo Levi's writing often does, or more explicitly, as Saul Friedländer does in *When Memory Comes*[3]—in any event viewing the past from a vantage point reached only at a distance from the events cited; the nonfictional fiction, which, whether written in the first person or in the third, claims or implies faithfulness to the historical record—at times by reciting the record itself—while simultaneously providing counterevidence that much else in the text is not, could not be, factual. So, for widely disparate examples, D. M. Thomas's *The White Hotel*, Leslie Epstein's *The King of the Jews*, Jean-François Steiner's *Treblinka*, Thomas Kenneally's *Schindler's List*, Elie Wiesel's *Night*, and Rolf Hochhuth's *The Deputy*. I quote (as typical of this genre) from the acknowledgments that precede a lesser-known "novel" that is in this respect, however, quite typical, Ursula Hegi's *Stones from the River* (1994):

My godmother, Kate Capelle, had the courage to answer questions I couldn't ask as a child while growing up in the silence of post–World War II Germany. . . . [She] broke the silence by documenting her memories of the war years on tape for me. Author Ilse-Margret Vogel . . . lent me photo albums of her childhood and offered valuable insights on what it was like to live in Germany between the two wars. Historian Rod Stackelberg trusted me with journals he wrote as a boy in Germany. Together with Germanist Sally Winkle, he guided me in my research. . . . My agent Gail Hochman, helped me with my research of Jewish traditions. Gordon Gagliano . . . advised me in matters Catholic and architectural.[4]

Readers of this preliminary statement who did not know that a novel was to follow might as readily anticipate a historical treatise; certainly

3. Saul Friedländer, *When Memory Comes,* trans. Helen R. Lane (New York: Avon, 1979).
4. Ursula Hegi, *Stones from the River* (New York: Poseidon, 1994).

there is an implicit commitment here to "truth telling" that goes well beyond accurately reporting the details of family structure or of religious rituals at a certain time in German history. And indeed, the writings that constitute this first group as a whole disclose a common commitment to historicity, however various the means by which they represent it—a commitment volunteered neither for literary reasons (what could these be?) nor for historical reasons (since then the genres would be quite different, those of history itself) but evidently (the one remaining alternative) for moral reasons. That is, as I shall be suggesting, out of deference for the subject or in order to preserve history, as the moral ground of memory would argue.

The second category—Holocaust writings that appear with only a subtext or context of historical reference—applies to a smaller but still substantial number of works whose indirection can be understood in terms of Aharon Appelfeld's aphorism that "one does not look directly into the sun" (i.e., *at* the Holocaust). Such works are exemplified, in fact, by the best-known of Appelfeld's own books, *Badenheim 1939*. For a reader who does not bring to that book prior knowledge of the Holocaust—the emergent threat of deportation for the Jews, their response of incredulity and denial, and finally the deportations themselves—it would almost certainly remain opaque, conveying the sense of a parable or allegory, but evasively and mysteriously because of the absence of the second, referential term presupposed in those literary genres. With such prior knowledge—which Appelfeld thus requires the reader to supply—the work is transformed. (One aspect of this issue is evident in the metamorphoses of the book's title: in the Hebrew original, the title was ironic, *Badenheim, Ir Nofesh* [Badenheim Spa or Badenheim Resort]; in the English, we have the quasi-historical *Badenheim 1939*; in the German, we have just the indefinite *Badenheim*. Appelfeld's German publisher feared fewer sales if "1939" were attached—exactly the opposite effect assumed for the English or American editions.)

To be sure, the diaries or memoirs or novels in the first group of writings mentioned also assume a subtext or context, but less as a literary or representational device than in the interest of literary economy; by contrast, in the second group of "indirect" Holocaust writings the unconscious of the texts—their repressed past—must be retrieved and articulated by the reader, with these acts themselves then integral in shaping the reader's response. Predictably, the largest proportion of writings here come from poetry, epitomized, it seems to me, in the *oeuvre* of Paul Celan but also, if somewhat less consistently because they are less oblique or "economical," in writers like Jacob Glatstein or Yehuda Amichai. Because the "condensation" notable among these—to use Freud's term from chapter 6 ("The Dream Work") in *The Interpretation of Dreams*—is typical of all poetry, one might object that there is nothing distinctive about its appearance in Holocaust poetry. But again, the condensation in Celan's "Todesfuge," for example, ensues not only in the general referentiality that virtually all discourse at some point depends on but also in the presupposition of a specific historical denotation that, to the extent that it remains unknown to the reader, will produce a radically different effect for him or her from the effect of the poem understood as a "Holocaust poem." (The emphasis that his readers placed on "Todesfuge" *as* a Holocaust poem eventually led to Celan's own estrangement from that piece; it arguably contributed more generally to changes in the way he shaped his later poetry.)

The third category of Holocaust genres—historical writing itself—may seem perverse or at best a conceit insofar as it characterizes the writing of history as a whole as a genre. Following the line of argument here, Holocaust history too becomes subject to the claims of the thesis proposed here earlier—and what could the claim that Holocaust *history* aspires to the condition of history possibly mean? But it is indeed the latter assertion that I introduce—in part against the conceptual background that discloses genres not as natural "kinds" but as themselves historical and conventional; more specifically, as an inference from the varieties of Holocaust history itself.

No one would dispute the large role of historical writing in articulating the complex events known—historically—as the Holocaust. Pick whatever angle of vision you will, and there are for it points of origin and confirmation in historical writing. From Gerald Reitlinger's early work *The Final Solution* to Hilberg's monumental study *The Destruction of the European Jews,* to Hannah Arendt's *Eichmann in Jerusalem* (and the numerous authors who have subsequently written *about* Arendt), to Martin Gilbert's compendious geographies (where geography too turns into history), to the *Historikerstreit* of Ernst Nolte, Andreas Hillgruber, Jürgen Habermas, Hans Mommsen, Martin Broszat, and others, to Saul Friedländer on the Vatican and Isaiah Trunk's *Judenrat*, and then to Robert J. Lifton's *The Nazi Doctors* (a plausible metonymy for the virtual library of writings about the conduct of the various professions in Nazi Germany), hardly an issue in the topology of the Nazi genocide and the culture sustaining it has not been worked seriously and deeply in the relatively short period (in historiographic terms) of fifty years. And there should be no doubt that as the Holocaust fades from first- or secondhand experience, the necessity of this historical writing as a ground for memory as well as knowledge—in effect, for everything written or thought about the Holocaust—will become ever more pressing.

Of course, the quantity of writing about a particular subject in a particular mode of discourse does not by itself argue for the distinction of a genre, let alone for applying that term to history as a whole on the basis of the small field of Holocaust history within it. For many historians, furthermore, to find the label *genre* attached to their work amounts to an attack on hard-won standards of evidence and proof that in their view are not functions of rhetoric or "style" at all. This is not the place to argue the issues strikingly defined by Hayden White in *Metahistory,* his study of nineteenth-century historiography; for the moment it will suffice to consider only the possibility of conceiving history as itself a genre of writing (as has been provocatively asserted by Richard Rorty for philosophy and by Thomas Kuhn, still more contentiously, for science).[5] To be sure, the evidence for thinking of history as a kind of writing goes beyond that provided by Holocaust history alone. But the evidence is plainly there as well, in certain large differences between the texts of Holocaust history—not about the data and events of the Holocaust, which in many instances have come to be regarded as beyond dispute, but in the emplotted representations of those data and events.

5. Hayden White, *Metahistory: The Historical Imagination in Nineteenth-Century Europe* (Baltimore: Johns Hopkins Univ. Press, 1974); Richard Rorty, "Philosophy as a Kind of Writing," *New Literary History* 10 (1978): 141–60; Thomas Kuhn, *The Structure of Scientific Revolutions* (Chicago: Univ. of Chicago Press, 1970).

I would support this claim with two examples from historians who are equally committed to the view that the Holocaust resulted from the conscious intentions of its perpetrators and who devote much of their work to the evidence leading to this conclusion but who, despite this common ground, nonetheless appear to inhabit different historiographic worlds. Consider first Raul Hilberg as he describes the "disappearance" of the German Jews from Germany—the progressive extermination of that population and the undeniable presence that the process would have had even for those who wished to avoid all knowledge of it:

> The [German] Jews deported to the Ostland were shot in Kaunas, Riga, and Minsk. Those who were routed to occupied Poland died there in the death camps at Kulmhof, Auschwitz, Belzec, Sobibor, Treblinka, and Lublin (Majdanek). Most of the Theresienstadt Jews who did not succumb in the ghetto were ultimately gassed in Auschwitz. For all the secrecy of the killing operations, the signs and signals of a drastic penetration permeated the entire Reich. Often the roundups of the victims were seen in the streets. If the seizures were unobserved, the apartments remained conspicuously empty. If the disappearance of the tenants was not noticed, there were stories and reports about the mysterious East.[6]

A rational, certainly coherent sequence presented without commentary or inflection—but not, of course, without an effect of enormous intensity. And now, Daniel Goldhagen, stressing the gratuitous, hence intentional brutality applied in the camps, exacerbated by the callousness of the guards:

> The Germans made love in barracks next to enormous privation and incessant cruelty. What did they talk about when their heads rested quietly on their pillows, when they were smoking their cigarettes in those relaxing moments after their physical needs had been met? Did one relate to another accounts of a particularly amusing beating that she or he had administered or observed. . . . It appears unlikely that these Germans lamented their vicious assaults on the Jews. . . . This community of Germans, many of whom had paired off in inti-

6. Raul Hilberg, *The Destruction of the European Jews* (New York: Holmes & Meier, 1985), 469.

mate relationships, flourished side by side with the hell for Jews, which these same Germans created and enthusiastically policed.[7]

It seems to me that the differences between these two passages provide evidence that historical writing itself aspires to the conditions of history. There can be little doubt that each of these passages has a rhetorical or suasive purpose; there may be some question, although there is nonetheless substantial evidence, that part of this purpose is held by the two authors in common. But there seems to me *no* question that historiographically—in the understanding toward which they urge their readers—the authors diverge sharply, Hilberg aiming to unite the historical representation with history itself, Goldhagen inviting his reader to an imaginary (in the event, prurient), if emblematic, encounter. The difference here, I believe, is between a conception of historical writing as a function of the understanding and a conception of history as a function of the will. Probably neither account is without some measure of what predominates in the other, but the difference in proportions is evident and, it seems to me, significant. Something in the way of an empirical test can be adduced here—in the prediction I would offer that readers for whom one of these passages carries conviction will be unmoved, even put off, by the other. And vice versa. Insofar as this is true, the argument for historical "styles" and thus also for history (including Holocaust history) as embodying variant conventions of genre becomes compelling. In these terms, then, history aspires to the actuality of history, since in its formulations not only is there no guarantee of success (and often evidence of failure) but there is the possibility at once of alternate emplotments or causal chains and of different kinds among these constructs.

It may be objected that in some sense all literary representation promises allegiance to history because any representation of character, or more largely, of human nature, will be measured by what is common and actual in human conduct. Even Aristotle's distinction be-

7. Daniel Jonah Goldhagen, *Hitler's Willing Executioners: Ordinary Germans and the Holocaust* (New York: Knopf, 1996), 339.

tween an impulse for the universal in poetry and for the particular in history leaves poetry still attached to history insofar as the universal encompasses the particular. Furthermore, the "universal" in this relation can at times reenter history, striking as sharply and contingently as any more designedly historical moment. Think, for example, of Lear on the heath carrying the dead Cordelia, a scene that forced even the indomitable Samuel Johnson away from the magic of art and back into the rush and stress of history: "I was many years ago so shocked by Cordelia's death, that I know not whether I ever endured to read again the last scenes of the play till I undertook to revise them as an editor." It is impossible to believe that the younger Johnson would have been comforted by a reminder that, after all, Cordelia didn't really die, that she was "only" an imaginary character in a dramatic fiction.

We may be tempted to recall that the issue noted here is common to virtually all literary representation. To make a place for Don Quixote and Gregor Samsa no less than for Lear, the imagination is required to supply much of the grist on which the mills of artistic laughter as well as pain depend. But even then history's infringement on art does not quite cease. To say that *King Lear* is about a king named Lear, or that the novel *Don Quixote* is about Don Quixote, is to say little indeed, and even that much is misleading. But to say of *Badenheim 1939* that it is about the Holocaust is to say something both true and literarily essential to a reading of the novel, bringing to bear on its understanding extraliterary details of which the novel itself, aside from its title with its own patchwork history, offers hardly a hint.

It might be argued that precisely because of this aura of the text that I suggest marks all the Holocaust genres, decisively in *Badenheim* and other works in the second group, but always to some extent, Holocaust writing as such turns out to have the features of a genre, albeit a minor one. The latter qualification precisely reflects and attests to that writing's dependence on history—another way, in terms of the account given here, of measuring the moral conditions to which Holocaust writing answers. Such a claim for the genre's minority status strikes more deeply, it should be evident, than the more typical and certainly more frequent abuses that run through much Holocaust writing of exploitative cant and sentimentality. (No doubt because of the subject, these seem more flagrant in Holocaust writing than elsewhere, although they do not differ essentially in kind.) For Holocaust writing and the subgenres into which it can be divided, the imagination is set within the limits of history, and it is constrained there by moral, not only aesthetic and not simply historical, conditions; they thus join, and for the same reason, other minor genres like the fable or the allegory.

A second objection to the account given might criticize its claims as obvious and, more damningly, trivial. Does not what has been said amount, after all, to the simple tautology that Holocaust writing has the Holocaust as its subject? But this formulation ignores the part of my thesis that asserts that more than occasioning Holocaust images, the historical Holocaust serves also as their "final cause"—that it is integral to what they aim at as history, even when the writing is fiction or poetry. Again, there is force to the claim that every act of representation or expression presupposes an extrarepresentational context, that is, that it appears against the background of what in an earlier and easier time would without embarrassment have been called reality. (It is obvious, often too obvious to be noticed, that persons represented in fiction or poetry have certain standard physical features and capacities except when there is a literary reason for their not having them—so, the metamorphosis of Gregor Samsa—and then too it is the contrast between historical normalcy and the deviation from it that matters.) From this point of view, then, there would be nothing distinctive in what has been claimed about Holocaust writing. But the divisions and examples of that writing as I have cited them provide evidence not only that they originate in the Holocaust but that they conclude there as well, by representing it, and doing so constantly under the shadow of a principle of historical authenticity. What stands as a plausible if risky conceit in Jean Baudrillard's book *The Gulf War Did Not Take Place* would become something quite different if his title (and work) had cited the Holocaust in place of the Gulf War. This does not mean that "Holocaust denial" can simply be legislated out of the artistic domain of Holocaust writing, but its absence from the long lists of Holocaust fiction is notable, and even more limited counterfactuals (like George

Steiner's discovery of Hitler alive in South America or Anne Frank's escape to a New England village in Philip Roth's *The Ghost Writer*) tread on dangerous ground.

A final and still more serious objection might accept my account for the sake of argument and then move to an obvious implication: if Holocaust genres aspire to the condition of history, would they not do better to *become* history (and their authors, then, historians)? One response to this has already been given: that history itself, even in its own terms, is not so readily actualized, as the differences between Hilberg and Goldhagen, for examples, attest. A second response comes from the combination of disinclination and incapacity described in the answer given this question by Cynthia Ozick, who has the powerful conscience of a Holocaust writer but a nonhistorian: that she would do history if she could, but she—the novelist—cannot. And a third response, which I only whisper here, half saying it, half not, is that indeed—apart from the question of how effectively they are able to do this—Holocaust writers who invite the imagination into their work and build on it should keep history always before them. On the traditional aesthetic requirement of an internal relation between form and content, is it not plausible to contend that the Holocaust, as subject or content, may be more responsive to certain forms, or genres, of expression than to others, and perhaps to some not at all?

The dangers that open at the edges of this last response are evident even in its most moderate formulation. I don't think that the claim is fully entailed by anything else I have said, but it has certainly been lying in wait there. And indeed there is something more to be said about why, if Holocaust genres do aspire to historical authenticity, as has been claimed here, that condition also *ought* to be the case. A shift, then, from form to norm, although based on two reasons that serve also as a directive for the Holocaust genres alluded to. The first of these is that the Holocaust ought to be written about—not only because it is aesthetically or historically evocative but also because of the moral ground that underlies those evocations. The second is that Holocaust writing has not been, and should not be, "about" the Holocaust by way of the imaginative permutations to which it, like any historical event, is open but because the events and character of the Holocaust require authenticity in its representation, that is, as history—not as historical or in the light of history or in the "style" of history. And this, again, neither for aesthetic reasons, since art is typically allowed great latitude ("poetic license") in the turns and twists it gives to history, with no possibility ruled out, nor for merely historical reasons, since then the Holocaust becomes but one item among an indefinite collection of data, perhaps placed—as it is in one encyclopedic version—between such alphabetically arranged entries as "Holmes, Sherlock" on one side and "Holy Grail" on the other.[8]

Is there such a thing as "mere" history, that is, history plain and simple? Yes and no—with both these characteristics affecting the aspiration of Holocaust writing. Yes, in the sense that for the basic historical unit of the chronicle all events are equal (thus, mere); no, in the sense that to the moral element of truth ingredient even in "mere" history is added the moral weight of certain particulars—the Holocaust, for one—which then have a voice, should have a voice, in their subsequent representations. In this there is not equality but difference, and a difference basic enough to produce deformations when it is denied or overridden. From this perspective, the fact-value distinction celebrated in contemporary scientific and philosophical discourse appears as a fiction, an obvious one even in its own terms once we credit the question of whether the distinction itself is a fact or a value.

There are practical as well as principled dangers in the legislation adopted in a number of countries (Canada, France, Germany) of legally prohibiting representations of the Holocaust that deny the occurrence of that event. (Some of this legislation is not directed specifically to the Holocaust but to "group libel" or to "incitement to racial hatred," although in each case the Holocaust has stood clearly in the background.) The moral basis of such legislation is substantial; I should argue that it applies, however, with only slight alteration not only to Holocaust denial but to Holocaust distortion, to Holocaust diminution, to Holocaust titillation, to Holocaust kitsch—examples of all of which are only too plentiful. Even in the most objectionable of these works an aspiration to historical authenticity is visible—dimly at

8. E. D. Hirsch, *The Dictionary of Cultural Literacy* (Boston: Houghton Mifflin, 1993).

times, at other times, even here, flagrantly. (Intention may have nothing to do with this; so, for example, the strong commitment to historicity of Holocaust denial, insofar as lying presupposes almost as strong a conception of truth as truth itself.) And again, it is this impulse for historical reference, I have been suggesting, that ought to underwrite Holocaust discourse, with the standard by which it is then to be judged (a necessary if not sufficient condition) being that of history as it sets limits for representations of the Holocaust. This, again, as fact and value are intertwined.

Let me bring this ascetic and meta- (in some ways anti-) aesthetic discourse to a consistently reactionary conclusion by citing two statements of testimony from, of all places, the brute world of chemistry. The first statement is by a purveyor of ironies who, as far as I have been able to determine, although living in its time, was largely untouched by the Holocaust and whose venture into chemistry was that of an urgently curious layman. The second is by a writer who lived directly in the worlds of the Holocaust and of chemistry and who, furthermore, discovered a connection between them. So, first, Roland Barthes—as he rejects the standard accounts that claim the historical precedence of painting (or the aesthetic impulse more generally) as inspiration for the "art" of photography, with its indisputable realism: "I say no, it was not the painters, it was the chemists . . . [who] made it possible to recover the rays emitted by . . . an object. The photograph is literally an emanation of the referent."[9] And then, Primo Levi as he reflects on his decision to become a student of chemistry at a time when the impending Holocaust was for him already a presence: "Chemistry led to the heart of Matter, and Matter was our ally precisely because the Spirit, dear to Fascism, was our enemy" ("Potassium"). "The nobility of Man acquired in a hundred centuries of trial and error, lay in making himself the conqueror of matter . . . and I enrolled in chemistry because I wanted to remain faithful to this nobility" ("Iron").[10]

9. Roland Barthes, *Camera Lucida*, trans. Richard Howard (New York: Hill & Wang, 1981).

10. Primo Levi, *The Periodic Table*, trans. Raymond Rosenthal (New York: Schocken, 1984).

You may by now anticipate the connection I would draw between these brief allusions to the hard science of chemistry and a science of the no less hard "matter" of history—the direct touch or "emanation of a referent" that is as directly implicated in Holocaust genres in my account of them as it is, for Barthes, in the "punctum" of photography. Certainly *The Periodic Table* and, even more severely, his more sustained memoirs of Auschwitz reflect Levi's attempt to confront the Holocaust in its "Matter," that is, from the viewpoint of a chemist of history: laboratory-neutral but bent fiercely to his analysis of stuff, with the Holocaust his scientific "unknown" to be broken down into its elements. Indeed, I offer a correspondingly empirical test for the characterization of Levi's writing as chemical: Would it make a large or a small or no difference to his readers if they should suddenly learn that his accounts of (or after) Auschwitz were not historically referential, chemical emanations but imagined—that is, fictional? Surely it is essential not only to his readers' emotional reactions but to their understanding that the "Matter" of his writing—what he alleges took place—should in fact have occurred. If what he wrote had not been experienced but imagined, the words of his text might not change in the slightest, but can there be any doubt of the difference that would, and should, make in the response of his readers?

Added to the other examples cited earlier in this discussion, this glance at chemistry and matter through the eyes of Barthes and Levi underscores the general claim entered here for the historical character —in aspiration and actuality—of Holocaust genres. That account constitutes, I believe, a response—indeed, an answer—to a troublesome inheritance, the still-present anxiety bequeathed by romanticism that art and its exemplars would not be able to survive the loss of their supposedly ahistorical transcendence. If ever there was a reason for taking matter, including the brute matter of history, seriously in itself and not merely as an occasion for moving on to a mystifying Other, surely the events of the Holocaust provide it—not because of the demands made by the writing of history for its own sake, but for the sake of that particular history and its demands, which, if not unique, are, I have been claiming, unequivocal.

There is no evidence in the array of Holocaust genres of their governance by an "invisible hand" that has directed them to a single end of the sort outlined. Yet they exhibit—at times despite themselves—a common extraliterary conscience, expressed, if not in a single voice, with the fine coordination of a chorus. Accidents like this don't just happen, and it is a measure of retributive, although not always poetic, justice that we should find in Holocaust genres a transitive principle: representation within the limits of history, history within the limits of ethics. This principle applies as a basis for judgment even when that judgment then proceeds to treat harshly some of the very works in which the principle itself is exhibited. This is, I suggest, a lesson we can learn from the Holocaust by the practice of history rather than by moralizing about it. For without history's often narrow, prosaic, nonironic, nonfigurative foundation, visible emblematically in its most rudimentary genre, the much-maligned "facts" of simple chronicle—who and how many did what to whom and how many and when—Holocaust writing and its genres, individually and collectively, would have been, and would be, merely imagined. And at this point, that possibility is and certainly ought to be unimaginable. Literally.

34

Holocaust Texts and the Blurred Genres | 2

Any reference now to "Holocaust writing" involves texts that number in the tens of thousands. The difficulty of characterizing that body of work as a whole and through the specific categories of genre is compounded by my use of *that* category (itself typically "blurred") to include as well "metagenres": the forms of discourse that distinguish historical and scientific discourse, for example, as these complement more standard literary genres like the novel or the short story, which themselves fall under the metagenre "imaginative writing."

But I nonetheless propose a specific thesis addressed to the array of texts in what may be called Holocaust writing, insofar as the Holocaust is a subject or theme in them. The thesis is this (in three clauses): that the more significant proportion of that writing stands in a subversive relation to the conventions of literary genre and even of metagenre; that the challenge to these conventions is itself a representational element in the works in which it appears; and that this blurring effect reflects two principal sources—the character of the Holocaust as a subject for literary representation and the role of historical and ethical causality in shaping the genres, and thus the forms, of literary discourse.

It seems obvious that the moral weight of its subject must be a factor in the blurring effect in Holocaust writing, if only because it is difficult to imagine any aspect of such writing for which the character of the Holocaust as a subject would not be a factor. Less obvious are the specific ways in which this ground assumes literary forms without leaving behind its combination of historical and moral reference. What emerge finally against this background, then, are genres acting in the role of moral and historical as well as aesthetic representation. This instance of the link between content and form is not in itself an innovation of Holocaust writing; any standard literary history will point the reader in the direction of numerous literary examples, if it does not always elaborate their theoretical substructure. And certain references to "transgressive" writing have become a critical commonplace in the recent migrations of poststructuralism. Holocaust writing, however, reveals systematic features of the blurring effect that are at once more innovative and more consequential than those evident in more "normal" appearances of writing, and this should not be surprising. Hard cases may make bad law, and they often also make bad writing. But they also afford an unusual grip or purchase on what the law—or the process of writing—is. Like stress tests in engineering, Holocaust writing pushes certain features of writing to their limits, in some cases to their destruction; arguably, then, what is disclosed from this source would be present, even if less evident or efficacious, when the subject represented did not exert the extreme pressure that the Holocaust does. In this sense, Holocaust writing affords a means of penetrating a literary unconscious—a subtext—active but less visible in writings about subjects whose moral and historical contexts are less pressing and so figure less prominently in their literary representations.

For evidence of this broad claim, I shall be referring to three examples, which come, respectively, from "imaginative" literature (what is usually called more flatly "literature"), history, and philosophy. Each of the examples contrasts two texts that disclose in their differences an issue of literary genre or convention and then, viewed together with the other pairs, advances the claim made here about the unusual strains on the use of "normal" genres in Holocaust writing. The texts cited are familiar and well established, although not undisputed and, more important for the present discussion, not so widely influential as to have displaced by the blurred conventions visible in them the older and more standard ones against which they are reacting.

The first of these pairs is the collection of short stories by Tadeusz Borowski published in English under the title *This Way for the Gas, Ladies and Gentlemen,* and Aharon Appelfeld's novel *Badenheim 1939.* Although in different ways, each of these reflects a basic unease—one might even speak here of a sense of inadequacy or, more extremely, of guilt—that affects much (and certainly the most accomplished) imaginative writing about the Holocaust. Among the sources of this unease, the most fundamental one appears as a doubting or disquiet in the act of writing itself, that is, in the writer's appeal to the imagination in the face of the literal, nonimagined fact of the Holocaust to which it is the author's evident purpose to give voice. The constant but unspoken question in these works is, What place can there be for the imagination or even for representation itself? What space is left for authors who commit themselves to images of a composite event so dense morally and historically as to leave the imagination little room in which to move or act?

In terms of literary conventions, what is at issue here is the broad line presupposed in virtually all literary genres and metagenres between historical and imagined reality—between the constraints of actuality, on the one hand, and the less restrictive domain of possibility, on the other. That this line is not impassable has been recognized as long as the distinction itself has been, beginning with Aristotle's first account of the difference between history and poetry. But these familiar qualifications have been insufficient to reassure Holocaust writing about the legitimacy of a role for imaginative discourse in the face of the unusual historical and moral weight it bears in the case of the Holocaust.

In much Holocaust writing this sense of inadequacy is openly expressed, almost as a standard trope, appearing in explicit acknowledgments, at times even as apologies by the author. In Borowski and Appelfeld the ambivalent form of address is both subtler and more fully realized imaginatively, but its presence is no less evident. Borowski's stories meet this issue head-on. For in contrast to the usual experience of reading, it is virtually impossible for the reader to decide from internal evidence alone whether those stories are fictional or not—with the insistence on that ambiguity itself integral to the representation. From one direction, Borowski introduces many standard features of historical writing, lingering, for example, on details of chronology, numbers, and causality that are typically excluded or much reduced in the short story; if only because of the limitations of space, the short story usually draws more heavily on associative images than enumeration. On the other hand, Borowski's narratives are unified internally with so little excess or irrelevance as to make them seem implausible as representations of the rough and unruly edges of history. And yet the incidents recounted in the narratives also suggest that history—experience in fact—is asserting itself: the immediacy of affect and the conviction conveyed by both event and language are so strong that even the most deliberate attempts of artifice to conceal its own presence would ordinarily fail to achieve them.

The effect is surrealistic, although quite different from the usual appearances of surrealism—including some that have the Holocaust as their subject, such as Jerzy Kozinski's *The Painted Bird,* or Jakov Lind's *Soul of Wood*—which typically depend on exaggeration or hyperbole for their effect. Borowski's surrealism could only be achieved, would probably only be attempted, where the literary subject was recognized and represented as itself so extraordinary that it could not be exaggerated, with that feature itself conveyed in the representation. Under these conditions, literary realism, which is rarely so realistic as not to reveal its own devices, becomes functionally indistinguishable from historical discourse, whether articulated in the first or third person (the implied authors of Borowski's stories variously appear in both these "persons"). It is as though for this subject the pressure of history is intense enough to deter the imagination, to inhibit its usual elaboration because it is superfluous: whatever it might accomplish has already been done for it. Here, in other words, where undermining the conventional line between fiction and nonfiction is itself part of the literary subject, exaggeration *is* realism.

In *Badenheim 1939* Appelfeld describes a vacation resort at the beginning of "the season." Strange occurrences begin to obtrude on the vacationers (as well as on the reader). The local band gives its daily concerts, the guests eat their strudel in the pastry shop. But the "Sanitation Department" initiates certain investigations, signs appear about the attractions of life in the East, the Jewish clients of the spa are singled out and required to register. At no point in the conjunction of these events, however, are reasons or explanations given; what is known from the text is only that the guests on holiday find their usual activities and pleasures interrupted, displaced, progressively infringed. As the novel closes, the vacationers have boarded a train that is to take them to the East, but what motivates this trip remains inexplicable for the vacationers and unstated for the reader. The vacationers find odd—deadly—reassurance in the fact that the cars of the train are dirty, uncared for; the journey, they infer, could not be a long one under those circumstances. And the reader? Well, the reader is obviously required to inscribe the omitted half of the novel; that is, its foundation, the historical framework that brings the author's "imagined" half to life.

The constant omission of literary causality in the sequence of its representation associates *Badenheim 1939* with the genres of allegory or the fantastic; Appelfeld himself has cited a large indebtedness to Kafka. But whereas in Kafka's *The Trial*, for example, the side of the allegory within the work is complete, the arbitrariness of Josef K's arrest and the proceedings against him being fully rendered, in *Badenheim 1939* the allegory stops just at the point where history, speaking through the reader, is required to complete the partial structure within the work. The publisher of the German translation of the novel realized this quite exactly when he dropped "1939" from the German title, a tactic, we surmise, that not only might get German readers into the novel—this was the evident purpose—but also, once discovered, would get them out of it more quickly than the publisher or the novel itself hoped for.

The common issue in these two books can thus be stated briefly: the conventions of the two imaginative genres to which, superficially, they respectively belong—the array of formal conventions designed to draw readers into an imagined world from which they then, under their own power, make their way through the fictions—are denied, subordinated to the constraints of history. History here, notwithstanding the supposed freedom of fictional worlds, has the last word—unspoken but insisted upon by the author and so then necessarily articulated, *written*, in the reader's own response.

The second pair of examples to be considered is from historiography: Raul Hilberg's *The Destruction of the European Jews* and certain of Martin Broszat's writings, principally his influential essay "Plea for a Historicization of National Socialism." The issue raised by these works is not a blurring of the genres independently in each but a challenge to the role of genre altogether, as Broszat represents that threat in the contrast he poses to Hilberg's book. (The latter is cited here as exemplary of one tradition of historiography of the Holocaust.)

Hilberg's work takes the form of a "trop-ic" model of tragedy. In this account there are in the unfolding of the "Final Solution" three principals: the perpetrators, the victims, and the bystanders. Like the chorus in Greek tragedy, the last of these is a textual surrogate for the reader as together they watch the rehearsal of a destruction unfold, complicated in scope, evoked to some extent by a latter-day equivalent to the "tragic flaw"—that is, the "anticipatory compliance" of the victims—but nonetheless directed and intentional and thus the responsibility of its main agents, the Nazis. The implied author in Hilberg's account distances himself from the account itself: there is no specific reference to moral enormity, no judgment in specifically moral terms. But this implied author has no need of them. The facts speaking for themselves are intended to define the tragic emplotment, and Hilberg employs a variety of stylistic devices, ranging from parataxis—short sentences unconnected by causal or conditional links—to elaborate nonnarrative charts that underscore the presence of an implied author who is undeniably "present" but who, by design and in the face of evident provocation, restrains himself from imposing on the material.

Yet the trop-ic structure emerges clearly, nonetheless—the more clearly, it might be claimed, because of the effectiveness of these distancing devices. And it is that trop-ic structure that Broszat challenges in his call for "historicization." What that term entails for him is a move to place the Holocaust within the broader context of German history and of history as such, and to do this, furthermore, by a localization of historical focus, a turn to *Alltäglichkeit*, the detail of everyday life in the period of National Socialism. The effect of the latter turn, as Broszat sees it, is to demythologize the history of the Holocaust, since what follows from the writing of history with this emphasis is an impression not of a unified or intentional design but of a multiplicity of individual occurrences and acts, often quite unrelated to each other. The outcome of the Holocaust is in these terms largely circumstantial in the strict meaning of that word: not accidental or uncaused, but unintended, produced by a convergence of factors that as a whole are without design. If the outcome of that convergence was moral enormity, and Broszat never denies this, it is not—could not be—tragic in the literary sense of that term and only by equivocation in its more ordinary usage. There are terrible "accidents," just as there are natural catastrophes with horrific consequences, but neither of these is *tragic,* and it is someplace between those two possibilities that Broszat's representation of the Holocaust would have a place.

In one sense, the difference between Hilberg and Broszat might seem to be a difference rooted in the facts themselves. This to a great extent would be how the authors themselves would understand the differences; that one writes as a Jew and the other writes as a German non-Jew would perhaps enter into this as well. But it is clear that what separates the two accounts is something more than their gathering of what are largely the same data. For when Broszat poses historicization as an ideal, the principal element that would then be challenged in Hilberg's account is not the accuracy of any particular fact or group of facts but the presence and role of historical intention altogether. It is likely, although not necessarily entailed, that Broszat would hold this to be a general feature of historiography; but in this account, at any rate, he in effect proposes the removal from the writing of history of its trop-ic character altogether, that is, its causality as a reflection (in part at least) of human agency. And it is just this boundary presupposition, not itself another historical fact, that underlies Hilberg's work, even as it professedly avoids ideology. It is this sort of presupposition, furthermore, that theorists like Hayden White ascribe to historiography as such in the claim that *any* emplotment of history embodies the structures of tropes and thus of agency, on the part of both the historian and the historical process.

For Broszat, who thus challenges the "meta-historical" view as such, there is no plot in the history of the Holocaust. And although he claims to base this conclusion on what the events in and leading up to the Holocaust disclose, it seems clear that his commitment to a method that makes the role of agency unlikely if not impossible undergirds this view. Broszat's challenge, then, is not only to one view of emplotting the Holocaust; it is to the conception of emplotment in history—if not as such, in much of it. The dispute (or *Historikerstreit*) in which Broszat's work figured, although immediately reflecting two opposed views of the Holocaust, was also a conflict about the writing of history: a challenge to the role of genre as a feature of historiography that was (against itself) dramatized by the issues at stake in writing Holocaust history.

The third case study to be considered consists of two philosophical works: *Lest Innocent Blood Be Shed*, by Philip Hallie, and *At the Limits of the Mind*, by Jean Amery. I characterize these books as philosophical, although readers will quickly discover that neither book has the standard features of philosophical writing as that is understood by most contemporary "professional" philosophers. So far as I have been able to determine, neither work was reviewed at the time of its publication in any American journal of philosophy, nor has either been cited subsequently in articles published in those journals. This blank space is obviously not a measure of quality, since bad books as well as good ones are reviewed and cited in those same professional publications. The likelier explanation is that the books by Hallie and Amery have not been considered to be philosophical works at all. But this, of course, is just the issue that their writings raise, a question that would not be settled—it would only be begged further—by citing credentials, for example, the fact that Hallie was indeed a professor of philosophy.

Any such judgment must finally be based on the writing itself, and there, it seems to me, except by arbitrary exclusion, the answer is clear. Certainly if one accepts the minimalist requirement repeatedly evident in the history of philosophical discourse, as it draws whatever lines can be drawn around recognizably general questions about, among other things, moral responsibility and obligation and how these concepts relate to theories of human nature, these works meet such requirements, although in unexpected ways. That is, they do so even though, and to an extent because, they challenge the conventions of philosophical discourse.

Hallie's book takes the form of a historical narrative describing the response of a French Huguenot village, Le Chambon, that sheltered Jewish children during the Occupation. The central figure in the narrative is the village pastor, Andre Trocmé, who organized the strong but nonviolent resistance that turned the village into a community. The issues that Hallie embeds in his narrative are familiar from the history of ethics: the connection between knowledge of the good and the motivation to act on that knowledge and the relation between individual character (good or bad) and the community to which the individual belongs. But these issues, which are evoked by the author's own view of what happened in Le Chambon—the book is subtitled "How Goodness Happened There"—are first evoked by Trocmé himself and the circumstances in which he and the villagers found themselves. The force of the questions raised depends on this narrative thread not accidentally or as exemplary but because they are unintelligible without it: it is the context that makes them possible (and in the context, necessary). The same questions, of course, might be articulated apart from this particular historical setting, but Hallie implies that it is indeed the setting he describes—and more generally, a *specifically* historical setting—that generates the questions; according to this view, such questions require a narrative substructure even to be fully understood, let alone answered. Put more concisely, moral questions *are* historical questions, presupposing individual human agency acting in a particular set of historical circumstances. This does not mean that there are no general or universal moral issues or principles, but that when such issues are viewed only or initially at that level, they remain abstractions and are therefore misleading. The most prominent example of this is Kant's categorical imperative, according to which universalizability becomes the test of moral validation for any particular action (and so, also for the agent), but which, as it is brought to bear on moral conflicts or dilemmas, has no means of proceeding further or, more tellingly, of understanding the specific conflict or dilemma itself.

Amery's book—which details a personal history that led from his role in the Belgian underground to his capture and torture by the

43

Gestapo and then to his deportation to Auschwitz—arrives at the general features of philosophical reflection by mingling the genres of autobiography and memoir. Read as history or, more narrowly, as memoir, Amery's account would join the large number of other first-person "survivor" narratives, which assume a fairly standard form. But philosophical reflection is entailed here not by the reader's empathy or association with the author but as Amery demonstrates the relation of the general to the particular: How would intellectuals, believers in the life of the mind, conduct themselves at the "limits of the mind," in Auschwitz? What is it that torture does to the body beyond the physical lacerations it inflicts? What does the process of alienation from a native ground and language mean for the definition of a self? Such questions can be posed in the abstract; it is essential for Amery's response to them, however, that any general answer presupposes a first-person account, not in addition to other evidence but because that first-person evidence is distinctive in its assertion and serves in effect as the basis for any subsequent, more general one. Obviously, third-person accounts have been written on the same topics. But not only is it unlikely that such accounts would have been written in the absence of the first-person accounts; there is a sense in which the former logically presuppose the latter. If there were no interior experience like that reflected on by Amery, what motive would there be for any of the external reports or descriptions?

To be sure, historical narrative and autobiography are familiar genres, but they are not familiar, certainly not currently, as genres of *philosophical* writing, which calls attention again to the larger thesis of the "blurred genres" around which the present discussion turns. The claim that the form of the two philosophers' works cited is evoked, even required, by their subject challenges two otherwise standard presuppositions of philosophical discourse. The first is that the form of philosophical writing is distinct from its content, that the very large variety of genres that "literarily" recur in the history of philosophy are thus accidental—in effect, that philosophy's history would not have differed significantly if it had been (or were now, retrospectively) laid out linearly, in texts consisting of a series of propositions that might be read as constituting a single large text, that is, the "book" of philosophy. The second assumption is that history *as* history does not matter to philosophical discourse, that since generality or universal principles, even a universal ideal language, are goals of philosophy, the study of philosophy would do well also to set out *from* them. This has in turn been taken to imply that examples cited as evidence within philosophical discourse would lose nothing if they were not historically referential but were contrived or made up. All that is required of philosophical evidence, in other words, is that it be possible, not actual; indeed, in these terms, examples that are historical open themselves to the charge of tendentiousness or special pleading. Or of exceptionality—of focusing on the exception, which then parodies rather than represents the rule. In either case, history as such is viewed as no aid to analysis, indeed as a possible impediment.

45

These assumptions are themselves embodied—represented—in the philosophical genre of the treatise or impersonal essay, which has become so dominant in modern philosophy as to be regarded as philosophy's natural or necessary medium—in effect, as not itself a genre at all. Some philosophical writing about the Holocaust—there has not been much altogether, but some of what there has been—has worked within the bounds of this genre, sometimes claiming the historical uniqueness of the Holocaust in a form that in its own terms contradicts the claim, sometimes reaffirming the conditions of that impersonal and deductive genre in its own assertions (for example, in arguing that for the traditional problem of evil, the Holocaust counts for no more than the most trivial instance of moral violation). From both these directions, all history becomes one—and in any event irrelevant to the writing of philosophy. This is indeed an arguable view of philosophical discourse, but one that is far from self-evident and is sharply and effectively disputed in the two works cited.

At least for the subject and the form of address articulated in these two books, philosophy is obliged to seek other means, to unsettle the conventions. That such other philosophical means are possible is demonstrated by what the books accomplish. (I do not mean to imply that aside from these examples or the topic of the Holocaust, philosophical writings do not, even today, employ a variety of genres, but there is no doubt that the "professionalization" of philosophy, especially in the twentieth century, has been the cause of a notable decrease in that variety.) Is it possible that the philosophical content of the two books discussed could be captured as well and as fully in a more standard philosophical genre or form? It is always difficult, of course, to prove the impossibility of an empirical claim; what is clear is that Hallie and Amery believed that there was an intrinsic and not only an incidental connection (e.g., a matter of taste) between the manner of their writing and the issues that engaged them bearing on the growth of the moral self—and that the differences between the respective genres in which they wrote and the more conventional ones employed in ethics and philosophical writing add force to their claims.

E V E N I F everything asserted so far about the blurring effect in the texts referred to were accepted for the sake of argument, how to account for it still remains a question. And here it seems to me that three principal explanations are possible. The first of these is that what characterizes the examples of Holocaust writing cited is not peculiar either to them or to Holocaust writing but a constant feature of literary history more generally. From the acknowledgment—hardly a matter of dispute—that all forms of discourse have histories of their own, coming into and (sometimes) passing out of existence, it follows that literary conventions and genres have been and will be in motion; this itself would assure a blurring effect in the history of discourse, even if it typically occurs in less dramatic and coercive circumstances than those of the examples cited here.

A second possible explanation is that the effect ascribed to Holocaust writing reflects the current suspicion in literary theory and cultural studies of not only all literary conventions but also categorial thinking as such. Put more summarily, that it would be exactly by such disruptive, even transgressive, means that postmodernism would confront the Holocaust. Constantly turning in that direction for far more ordinary occurrences, that theoretical impulse would *a fortiori* do so in reacting to the Holocaust and the historical rupture it caused.

Either or both of these explanations undoubtedly contribute to the phenomenon of the blurred genres in Holocaust writing; more generally, it seems obvious that even Holocaust writing could not expect to detach itself from the history of writing as such. No revisionist means of writing could "break the vessels," much as they might sometimes wish or attempt to escape the history of discourse and the constraints that it has set up even for those who rebel against it. The genres of Holocaust writing, in their efforts to disrupt or revise the traditional genres, nonetheless reflect them in those same efforts; this is a constant and not insignificant element in Holocaust images of all kinds.

A third possible explanation seems to me the most compelling: that with this disruption of traditional genres, Holocaust writing reveals the conventions that have shaped those genres and metagenres as having a moral and historical ground, which then openly becomes integral to their literary or aesthetic representation. No doubt, in this respect as in others, the Holocaust as a subject of representation makes unusual demands in its role as a subject of discourse. This does not mean that the same grounds are not present when the demands are less severe, but only that the conventions of genre are better able under ordinary circumstances to conceal their origins and intentions, to achieve the desired effect of art concealing art. In such cases neither historical fact nor ethical judgment exerts nearly the same force. The blurring of genres in Holocaust writing, then, is another and harsh way in which the alleged distinction between content and form is shown instead to be a function of their relatedness—further confirmation, if more were needed, of the sources of literary form in extraliterary content.

Before closing, it seems necessary to mention a last issue that cuts across genres, indeed across the theoretical status of genres as such; in this sense it is also marginal to the present discussion, although, I should argue, significant for the topic of Holocaust writing as such. It bears specifically on an issue that is constantly pushed aside in the discussions of Holocaust writing—namely, literary or aesthetic evaluation—and still more narrowly on the topic of what we might call, unfashionably and directly, "bad" writing. Ordinarily, to characterize a literary work in these terms, especially if there is general agreement about it, would also be to conclude the discussion. There would be little more to say about the text in question, except perhaps to advise against bothering to read it or to recommend against writing like it.

To be sure, a popular anthology of bad poetry has been published *(The Stuffed Owl),* and at least one course in a well-known department of comparative literature entices students with the title "Bad Literature." More usually, however, it would be assumed that there is little to be gained by reading or studying bad writing, except (again) to provide examples for the pathologies on display in composition courses, and then with a therapeutic rather than a readerly purpose. This dismissal is usually defended on practical grounds—that there is little enough time to read or teach good or "great" literature—and so here critical taste and pedagogical obligation for once coincide. Better simply to let bad literature alone.

But this view of bad writing and the role of criticism in respect to it seems inadequate in respect to bad Holocaust writing, at least on the basis of the claim that much of *this* bad writing may nonetheless have good effects. To be dismissive in the way described above is to hold that the writing is without value or even harmful, that it might be better if the texts in question were not read, or more strongly, if they had not been written. And indeed, few readers of Holocaust writings would deny that there is much "bad" writing among them: novels, poems, plays, memoirs that display some or all of the many features readily agreed on as objectionable—sentimentality and cliché, exploitation and tendentiousness, in short, literary and moral dishonesty. (This is not to mention the more extreme writings on the boundaries, the sub-genres of concentration camp pornography or historical revisionism, which denies that the Holocaust occurred.) Even the most conventional and recognizable genres—the novel, poetry, docudramas, movies, psychological, philosophical, and historical studies or memoirs—may and at times have distorted or subverted the subject of the Holocaust, appearing then as expressions of self-indulgence, emphasizing the pathos of the author or the characters he or she deploys, with the effect of distorting or subverting and certainly diminishing their subject. Nor is such abuse restricted to "imaginative" writing, since at the other end of the spectrum the systematic abstractions of philosophy, theology, and the social sciences have also proved capable of falsification, first and mainly in the leap from the particularity of the Holocaust (in that "special" relation between perpetrators and victims) to the generality of humankind or human nature, reflecting on the Holocaust as if it had been a class in elementary ethics or psychology. There is much that can and ought to be said about the egoism and cruelty of human nature, the thin veneer that separates civilization from barbarism—but no specific reference to the Holocaust is required for such reflection. Even the occurrence of the Holocaust would not necessarily be decisive in assessing the balance of evidence considered in reflecting on such topics.

Yet at least some of the writings that fully warrant such objections have arguably also been effective in calling public attention to the phenomenon of the Holocaust, in conveying information about it at least in a general form and perhaps also—this is more difficult to prove—in shaping moral responses and attitudes about the Holocaust and, arguably, about ethical issues more generally. One example often cited of this possibility is Gerald Green's television series *Holocaust,* which in standard critical terms was found severely wanting yet had remarkable public appeal in the United States and abroad, perhaps most notably in (then) West Germany. Other writers or works or "productions" might be similarly characterized. If there was somewhat more evenly balanced critical disagreement about William Styron's novel *Sophie's Choice* and Steven Spielberg's film version of *Schindler's List,* the general issue was much the same; clearly it can and should be separated from the judgment of any particular works. That issue, again, is tied to what has emerged as a significant pedagogical function of Holocaust writing (in all its genres), a function that, although it applies to other writings and their subjects as well, gains in importance here as the subject adds weight to the twofold function: first, by representing the *fact* of the Holocaust and, second, by bringing that fact to the attention of a broad and diverse public who might otherwise know little about it. Neither of these is a necessary or even common purpose of most other writing in respect to its subjects or contents. More usually—certainly this is the case with imaginative writing—there is no particular historical event to which it answers, and authors themselves come to accept, however grudgingly, the usually limited publics who find them out. Insofar as Holocaust writers wish in common to emphasize the occurrence and moral weight of the Holocaust, to make these known to audiences of very different kinds, including readers who might be resistant together with those who are simply indifferent, there would also be an arguable social and pedagogical justification for such writings, irrespective of how bad—sensationalist, mawkish, triumphalist, historically problematic—it is. Such reasoning would not, to be sure, make bad writing good, but it might well make it justifiable or, even more strongly, necessary, in any event more important or valuable than the "good" in some good writing. This possibility suggests that as the genres of Holocaust writing may be blurred under the moral and historical weight of its subject, the same reaction may also extend to the genres of critical thought and writing *about* that writing.

The Limits of Representation and the Representation of Limits | 3

The reference in my title to "limits" of representation might seem to imply that limits themselves are not representations. Since the question I will mainly be addressing is whether or where there are limits beyond which representations of the "Final Solution" cannot or should not go, those limits evidently would not at the same time be themselves within the area "represented." And indeed, the issue tendentiously posed in this way is one of substance as well as logic. By definition, there must be a difference between a representation and its object *un*-represented, with the former adding its own version to the "original" it represents. In this sense, the opposite of *representational* is not *abstract* (as applied, for example, to nonrepresentational painting) but *literal*, the object as it is before or apart from being re-presented.

There is, furthermore, a tacit suffix attached to all instances of representation. Representations are characteristically representations-*as*, with that locution implying the existence of other possible "representations-as." So, for example, the French Revolution could be "represented-as" or "as-not" having been a true class struggle—with no option in either version, however, of escaping the qualifying suffix. A space obtrudes here between an object or event and its representation, allowing, indeed requiring, choices among the alternatives for which the space clears a way. Any representation, then, in addition to its more manifest content, entails and so also represents the exclusion of at least some other possible ones. No representation, then, without duplication, or at least without other possibilities.

This native pluralism—to that extent, also skepticism—in the practice of representation suggests an antagonism between it and the concept of limits, since the role of limits is presumably not to multiply alternatives but to restrict them, in effect to say no. Indeed, the tension between representation and limits comes to light in the status of the limiting term *no* itself—a point suggested by the question for grammar of what "part of speech" that term is. Typically, the so-called parts of speech are understood representationally—verbs as representing actions, nouns as representing objects, and so on—but there is no corresponding group-likeness with which the term *no* can be associated. The dictionary, with customary assurance, identifies it as an adverb, that is, as a representation of "how" events occur. But even this authority does not quite dispel the sense that the limit asserted in a flat denial requires a category equally flat or one-dimensional, a category so single-minded that unlike other parts of speech, whichever one it is may not be representational at all.

Yet it is also evident that few limits do say no unequivocally. More often what they exclude is already present or implied, not just in the saying but in fact. For most limits that are asserted, other possibilities can be readily imagined; for many of *these,* an alternative to the limits asserted is not only imaginable but actual. Limits are invariably asserted, in fact, in the presence of transgression, after—and, arguably, because —violation has occurred. Indeed, the representation of limits —the form that limits take as related to the function they serve—is usefully understood at its origins in relation to the phenomenon of transgression. This relation is also pertinent, in certain respects crucial, for characterizing the limits that constrain historical and literary accounts of the "Final Solution," which are the representations to be considered here.

One formal consideration may be brought up about both the "limits of representation" and, in my reversal of that phrase, the "representation of limits." In each case, limits are referred to as if given—as though, notwithstanding disagreements about what or where they occur, there could be no question that they exist. But this implication might be better understood as no more than a manner of speaking, in the way that religion or morality, quite real in terms of social causality, turn out, in certain accounts, to be large-scale fictions. Viewed from this perspective, the occurrence of limits would be recognizable as a representation of something else, for example, of a psychological or even biological impulse for boundaries or taboos, perhaps even of an intrinsic incompleteness in all systematic structures. Those two "deep" versions of limits are neatly joined, as it happens, in Mary Douglas's description of the recurrence in cultural structures of the phenomenon of pollution. "Where there is dirt, there is system," her epigram on this goes. "Primitives and moderns, we are all subject to the same rules."[1]

Even this general claim, however, does not explain the specific forms that limits take or the processes that lead to them in the space of the imagination. In that space the possibility that limits are not more than artifacts, freely chosen, perhaps self-consuming—in effect that for the imagination there are no limits—is proposed as a condition. Thus, for example, Leonardo da Vinci, in a well-known passage from his *Treatise on Painting,* offers advice to the aspiring artist:

You should look at certain walls stained with damp, or at stones of uneven color. . . . You will be able to see in these the likeness of divine landscapes, adorned with mountains, ruins, rocks, woods, great plains, hills and valleys in great variety; and then again you will see these battles and strange figures in violent action, expressions of faces and clothes. . . . In such walls the same things happen as in the sound of bells in whose stroke you may find every named word which you can imagine.[2]

Leonardo then goes on to caution the artist about the practical labor that remains for him after he "sees" the landscapes or faces in the stained walls and colored rocks. But the representations identified by

1. Mary Douglas, *Purity and Danger* (Harmondsworth: Penguin, 1970), 48, 53.
2. Leonardo da Vinci, *Treatise on Painting,* trans. A. Philip McMahon (Princeton: Princeton Univ. Press, 1956), 50.

Leonardo themselves serve as emblems of representational freedom. When walls and stones yield the variety he details, there could hardly be limits hindering anything else discerned there; where the imagination is set in motion, we infer, anything can come to represent anything else and, conversely, any representation can have anything else as its object or occasion.

The extreme possibilities, then, are marked. On the one hand, limits exist because they must: human culture or consciousness or perhaps even biology cannot do without them. On the other hand, limits—at least the limits of representation—are at most conventional and thus open to continual, ultimately limitless variation if only because there is nothing to prevent this, no imaginative "natural kinds." (Since any specific representation must turn out to be limited, it would in these terms also be unnatural.) Although the general force of these extreme and contradictory positions suggests their own status as a priori and so beyond argument, what is clearly not beyond discussion is the fact that most representations of limits stand between those extremes. The examination of limits in this middle ground may be informative about the extremes as well, although even without this, such scrutiny will disclose the role of limits in practice—the point at which the representation of limits begins to shape the limits of representation.

Transgression and Representation

I refer to the unlikely conjunction of transgression and representation in a strong sense: transgression as a condition for representation. Once again, the phenomenon of artistic representation illustrates the claim, as in Heinrich Wölfflin's assertion of the limits that circumscribe the development of artistic style: "Not everything is possible," he writes about that history, "at every time,"[3] in effect denying the artist at a particular moment what later or earlier would be an artistic option. It should be noted that the limits thus posited by Wölfflin constrain not only what can be painted at a given time but what the artist at that

3. Heinrich Wölfflin, *Principles of Art History*, trans. M. D. Hottinger (New York: Dover, 1950), ix.

point is capable of imagining. There could be no representation of the limits that apply here, since to identify their terms would be already to transgress them; for the artist to conceive what he cannot do—to imagine what he cannot imagine—would be to have gone beyond the limits. Even the characteristic estrangement or defamiliarization ascribed to art by the Russian Formalists would not be an exception to this nonrepresentational limit; it too, after all, is a literary counterpart to the phenomenon of transgression or violation.[4] In such formulations the relation between transgression and representation is posed negatively, with no possibility of arriving at a representation of the limit except by transgressing it. Yet this means again that the limit by itself is posited without representation.

It may be objected that this example depends heavily on one view of art history, and a disputed one at that. But an analogous argument for the relation between transgression and representation appears just as emphatically in the Aristotelian "law" of contradiction. In Aristotle's own terms, the assertion that something cannot both be and not be itself in the same respect at the same time cannot be denied without presupposing that assertion itself. The limit posed, in other words, cannot be transgressed; at least, to do so would occur not humanly but, as Aristotle concludes, in the life of a vegetable.[5] In this example as in the first one, then, transgression is not only impossible in fact but unimaginable—incapable of representation because of the implicit exclusion of alternatives. The assertion of the limit here is thus not representational but literal or iconic, pointing only to itself.

The form of the relation thus asserted between transgression and representation is not the only one available to the relation; three alternative permutations of the two variables are also possible. As the transgression of its limits is judged (in the examples already cited) as (1) impossible and unimaginable, transgression can otherwise be seen as (2) imaginable but impossible; (3) unimaginable but possible; or (4) imaginable and possible. Although like the first, the second and third of

---

4. See, e.g., Victor Shklovsky, "Art as Technique," in *Russian Formalist Criticism,* ed. Lee T. Lemon and Marion J. Reis (Lincoln: Univ. of Nebraska Press, 1965), 13ff.

5. Aristotle *Metaphysics* 1006a–1009a.

The Limits of Representation

these conceptions are only indirectly pertinent here, they too underscore the relation claimed between transgression and representation. The second option mentioned is exemplified in physical limits, in the "law" of the conservation of energy, for example, or in the limit defined by the speed of light. Such limits assert the physical impossibility of transgression, but the limits pose no barrier (presumably even for those who fully understand their grounds) to imagining such violation—the existence, for example, of a particle that moves at 187,000 miles rather than 186,000 per second (insofar as *that* can be imagined). But here as in the first version of the relation between transgression and representation, no special constraints apply to historical representation: such physical limits would presumably apply as well to both past events and their present representations. And although it is possible to write about (or imagine) a historical event in terms that violate recognized physical limits, nothing more than that would have to be known in order to discredit such accounts. (Anachronisms, for example, cannot accurately represent the past.)

The third relation cited between transgression and representation may seem puzzling or self-contradictory: how can the transgression of a limit be possible and yet unimaginable? Although the conjunction here strains intelligibility, it is by just this combination of features that Kant defines the Sublime. In that conception, the recognition of a transcendence that, because of its limitlessness, cannot be represented impels the experience, distinguishing it from the more conventional (limited) aesthetic judgment with which Kant contrasts it.[6] So, in his example, the limitlessness of the power and expanse of the ocean cannot itself be represented, but the viewers' recognition of that limitlessness attests to their capacity for going beyond all physical limits (including their own). A relation is thus claimed between the possible and the unimaginable, with the transgression of limits once again at the basis of their definition.

(To anticipate a point to be elaborated later: For Kant and the tradition following him, the "fact" of the Sublime exalts the human subject as a moral agent—that is, the moral self unlimited as moral—but

6. Immanuel Kant, *Critique of Aesthetic Judgment*, sec. 28.

with no suggestion of anything analogous that applies to acts of moral enormity. Yet Kant's conception of "radical evil" [e.g., in the *Groundwork*] approximates an inversion of the Sublime that, joined to the historical evidence, might well characterize the Nazi genocide—as moved by an impulse not only to transgress limits but to deny that such limits apply at all. Transgression "downward" would, in these terms, be a counterpart to the "upward" move of the Sublime.)

This version of the relation between transgression and representation itself evokes the fourth alternative cited, since it is here, in the transgression of limits as both possible and imaginable, that the conception of limits as moral comes fully into view. The reason for locating moral limits under this heading will be evident: historically as well as psychologically, the representation of such limits assumes the actuality, not just the possibility, of transgression. The possibility is presupposed if the limits are to be at all relevant, since without this possibility, reflected in the role attached by moral deliberation to free will, adherence to a limit could have no moral weight. (The conception of a limit would here be a parody—like drawing a bull's-eye on a target after the arrow had hit it.) The *actuality* of transgression, in contrast, is presupposed in identifying a specific limit. That the determination of this point may be a matter of convention does not mean that it is arbitrarily chosen; on the loosest view of the functional strategies of culture, limits would hardly be asserted unless the practice prohibited had occurred in fact. So, for example, Fernand Braudel, the historian of everyday life, traces the spread in the Arab world of the dangerous new substance coffee and deduces one particular turn of that history: "[We know that] it had reached Mecca by 1511 since in that year its consumption was forbidden there."[7] Transgression figures here as a condition for the representation of limits, a condition that for Braudel is doubled in its occurrence: once in Mecca, before the prohibition was formulated, and once in Paris, as the historian rehearsed it. First, then, as a condition for limits, and second as a condition for the history of limits.

7. Fernand Braudel, *The Structures of Everyday Life*, trans. Sian Reynolds, vol. 1 (New York: Harper & Row, 1982), 256.

The Limits of Representation

A Moral "Radical" of Historical Representation

To ask about the limits that apply to representations of the "Final Solution" is minimally to refer to that event in historical terms. It is clear that those terms and what they denote have to be imagined. Indeed, the challenge to conceptualization and to language in the Nazi genocide is undeniable, applying to its initiators as well as to those of us who now reflect backward on it; consider only the complex although brief history of the term *genocide* itself.[8] It is unlikely, however, that we would be inquiring now about the limits of representation in respect to the "Final Solution" if its representations were regarded only as fictions. The fourfold schema outlined above, of limits as reflecting the relation between transgression and representation, thus impels the question of which among the four options is the most adequate basis for marking the limits of historical representation.

I have already suggested that the first alternative, where transgression affirms or presupposes the limit transgressed, would not apply to historical representation more than to any other; here as elsewhere, logic is historically indifferent. Nor, for most historical claims, whether at the level of chronicle or of interpretation, would even extreme alternative versions be precluded by limits of physical impossibility. No evident physical necessity blocks the reflection that Caesar might not have crossed the Rubicon—and a historical narrative that took that scenario seriously might well illuminate the accepted but different account. For reasons already given, moreover, the category of the Sublime, viewed either straight on or inverted—transgression as possible but beyond representation—would be applicable to historical assertion only after authentic limits had first been defined that the "Historical Sublime" might then challenge.

By a process of exclusion, then, if limits hold for historical representation at all, they appear first in the fourth version cited, where transgression is both imaginable and possible. The example to be elaborated of this relation invokes the representation of both moral and

8. On language as a factor in the "Final Solution," see Berel Lang, *Act and Idea in the Nazi Genocide* (Chicago: Univ. of Chicago Press, 1990), chs. 1 and 4.

historical limits. This is, I hope to show, not an ad hoc or arbitrary conjunction; the connection between the two is intrinsic, and even when its role as representation is relatively unimportant, it is nonetheless present. Indeed, it is on the basis of this connection that the applicability of limits to representations of the "Final Solution" comes most clearly into view.

The connection of moral to historical representation can be made evident on two levels. The first level is that of historical chronicle. The assertion—or its denial—that on 20 January 1942 certain members of 59 the Nazi hierarchy, meeting at Wannsee, discussed the terms—and the term itself—of the "Final Solution" is separable from other explanatory or causal accounts that might be required to elaborate it. Admittedly, the criteria to which even the bare assertion answers presuppose a conception of evidence and to that extent also of interpretation; such presuppositions also bear on the question of why that event rather than another should be remarked. But what is asserted or rejected in the "genre" of the chronicle does not, I should argue, require contextualization or a narrative account that extends beyond its own grounds. In this sense, the chronicle is, systematically, a point-zero in historiography; any disagreement about its assertions is in principle subject to adjudication in the terms of chronicle itself.[9]

Against the background of recent literary and aesthetic theory, I am aware of the risk in positing this (or any) foundation for a form of discourse. It is clear, moreover, that the chronicle itself is a literary "genre," assuming certain conventions that are also representations; like facts in scientific discourse, the chronicle in historical writing follows from a process of abstraction. But to admit these qualifications, conceding also that items cited in a chronicle may in that context have suasive purposes as well as others, does not mean that their appearance is exclusively rhetorical or inexplicable apart from a larger "metanarrative." If historical representations are at all distinguishable from those of fiction, the difference is located here, at the level of chronicle, if only *faute*

9. The proposal made here draws on Hayden White, "The Value of Narrativity in the Representation of Reality," *Critical Inquiry* 7 (1980): 5-27, although altering the relation defined there between "annals" and "chronicles."

de mieux. (The fictional analogue to the temporal references of chronicle is an atemporal constant: "Once upon a time. . . .") To be sure, the items constituting the chronicle can be challenged. But what is in dispute in these cases is of a different order from what might occur at the second, narrative level of historical statement, which builds on (and presupposes) the citations of the chronicle. Consensus at the level of chronicle leaves open the possibility of divergence beyond it, but both consensus and disagreement differ in significance, depending on which of the two levels they appear at.

The foundational role this ascribes to the genre of the chronicle appears with unusual force in representations of the "Final Solution" because of the way those representations build on the absence of certain details of chronicle, an absence then reflected in significant differences in the second-level, or narrative, accounts of that event. Most notable here in the historiography of the Holocaust is the absence of, or at least the failure so far to locate, a specific "Führer order" that, recorded as chronicle, would provide a basis for representing historically the second-level, causal development of the "Final Solution." The familiar Functionalist criticism of Intentionalist accounts of the "Final Solution" originates here, contesting the Intentionalist willingness to posit an overall shape for genocidal intention that assumes a prior act of the sort that the explicit order by Hitler (if it existed) would be. Systematically, the failure to discover the latter order has been the basis for the Functionalist accounts that still pose the weightiest alternative to Intentionalist representations and that, from the tension thus created, led to the *Historikerstreit.* It might be possible, even with the discovery of a "Hitler order," to argue for the Functionalist representation of the "Final Solution" as an incremental process impelled by independent, sometimes competing forces within the Nazi hierarchy, of which the Hitler order would then be only one among several; but this account would then be more difficult to defend.[10]

10. On the issues of fact-finding and differences in interpretation between the Intentionalists and the Functionalists, see, e.g., the exchange between Saul Friedländer and Martin Broszat, "A Controversy about the Historicization of National Socialism," in *New German Critique* 44 (1988): 81–126; Eberhard Jäckel, *Hitler in History* (Hanover, N.H.: Univ. Press of New England, 1984), 29–46; Christopher R. Browning, "The Deci-

Much can be said, of course, about other aspects of the two conflicting second-level accounts thus recognizable as Intentionalism and Functionalism, but for the moment I focus only on one of these, namely, how they bear on the question of whether and how responsibility is to be ascribed for the "Final Solution." The differences in possible responses to that question obviously have significant consequences, not least as certain Functionalist accounts have urged that the facts of the Nazi genocide should "go away"—be absorbed in the longer and naturalized view of German history. And indeed, if the "Final Solution" had been due to structural conditions rather than to someone's, or some group's, intentions, then of course it should be possible to naturalize it, to put it aside once the conditions that produced it were changed. Are such differences in consequence—*present* history—pertinent to the way the history of the past should be written? There can be little doubt that they do affect the writing of history, and in what I call a Moral "Radical" of Historical Representation there would be a basis for this connection in the elements of historical representation itself, specifically in the relation there between fact and value.

The formula for the Radical of Historical Representation posits a factor in variant historical accounts of the "same" event based on the moral consequences of the respective accounts. The formula thus entails that the burden of evidence incurred in choosing between different historical representations will increase, first, in proportion to the "factual" distance between the representation chosen and those rejected and, second, as that distance is multiplied by a moral "weight" assigned to the issue at stake among the variant accounts. In its mathematical form, this would be $R = (A^1 - A^2) \times W$. How the "moral weight" is to be determined is not part of the formula, although I describe below the way it emerges as a function of the moral community in the context of which the judgment is made.

An example of the Radical of Historical Representation at work can be found in the evidentiary distance separating the Intentionalist and

---

sion Concerning the Final Solution," in *Unanswered Questions*, ed. François Furet (New York: Schocken, 1989), 96–118; and Charles S. Maier, *The Unmasterable Past* (Cambridge: Harvard Univ. Press, 1988).

Functionalist accounts of the "Final Solution." The disagreement between those accounts does not occur at the level of chronicle: the Functionalist position need not and generally does not entail a denial that genocide or at least mass murder was an outcome of Nazi acts, however uncoordinated or collectively unintended—or even, in Ernst Nolte's extreme version, excusable and perhaps, although he does not *say* this, obligatory—those acts allegedly were. The differences between the two positions arise, then, even in explaining the apparent absence of the Führer order, at the second level of interpretation; it is there too that the differences in consequence of the two conflicting accounts— the differences summarized in the Radical of Historical Representation —become clear.

It has been amply demonstrated that a strong moral tension underlies the differences between the Intentionalist and Functionalist accounts and in the *Historikerstreit* more generally, even in the aspects of these disagreements that do not bear directly on issues of intention or responsibility. Understood in terms of the Radical of Historical Representation, this moral tension is not adventitious but intrinsic. I do not mean to imply by this that the moral weight of issues like the question of responsibility, on which second-level historical accounts often disagree, *by itself* should determine the content of historical representation; terrible outcomes may occur with no human agency at all. But the judgments incorporated in such representation ought to include reference to moral decisions that affect the event now represented. This factor of moral judgment on the part of the historian—what might be called "the historian's risk"—is then ingredient both in the representation and in the criteria by which it is subsequently measured.

The differences that stand to be revealed by such analysis in the "nest" of differing representations of the "Final Solution" come most blatantly to view, of course, in the "Holocaust denial" claim that goes beyond the Functionalists to deny not only intentionality but the very phenomenon of genocide or mass murder in the Nazi period. In terms of the Radical of Historical Representation, the distance (and risk) between competing representations increases from a starting point in Intentionalism to that defined by the differences between Intentionalism and Functionalism and then, to the other end of the spectrum, where the alternative posed in historical representation is not whether mass murder occurred by design but whether it occurred at all. But if it seems obvious at this extreme point that the representational difference involves more than simply a determination of "matters of fact," the difference is a function not of this one position alone but of historical judgment as such, whatever form it takes. Being right or wrong about the chronicled matters of fact in conflicting historical accounts has a moral weight that marks the representation that is on this basis then elaborated or "chosen" by the historian among the possibilities open at that point. In an extreme example of such choice, the decision would be confronted here whether the "Final Solution" had been implemented or not. What is at stake in that decision is, it seems evident, more than only the recognition or denial of certain facts of the matter; the decision is also a moral one, reflecting also the nature of what is being decided.

To be sure, even a large increase in the burden of evidence as measured in terms of the Radical of Historical Representation would not imply that a limit of representation had been transgressed. But it does indicate how such a limit might emerge, and it shows what the transgression would amount to. Indeed, as the distance between alternative representations increases, a representation that does not incorporate recognition of this fact—not simply by describing the difference but by basing the proportions of the representation on it—seems to violate a twofold limit: a formal limit of difference (by treating all possibilities of chronicle as equal) and, for the example cited, the limit (and weight) required by the "Final Solution" itself (by falling short of it).

Representation and the Moral Community

The question remains of how the moral significance claimed for matters of fact in the Radical of Historical Representation is to be determined, and I mention here only one principal factor that is involved, namely, the role of the moral community. I mean by *moral community* that the moral weight ascribed to a description or explanation analyzed in terms of the Radical reflects the context of social proximity or identity in which the historical representation is addressed (in the present, that is, rather than in the past represented). In one sense, this claim may seem to go without saying: of course we speak in the here and now. Yet there will also be widespread agreement against the first acknowledgment, on the grounds that the moral quality of an act ought also to be judged apart from any particular historical or social context; the distance separating the present from the age of the Caesars, for example, hardly alters the evildoing of a Caligula or a Nero. Nor is there a plausible way morally to distinguish among like instances of wrongdoing, even of murder and even in terms of numbers (the moral difference between someone's, or some group's, responsibility for the deaths of a thousand people in "contrast" to nine hundred would escape any moral calculus except a narrowly utilitarian one). Yet it is also undeniable that the lives or deaths of relatives and friends differ in their effects on us from the lives or deaths of others; events embedded in social identity or proximity consistently reflect that identity in the significance associated with them.

It might be objected that even if the latter claim is true psychologically and historically, the analogy it claims is inadequate morally: the weight attached to a wrong should not depend on the time or place at which the wrong is committed or on the particular persons or groups affected by it. This tension between the universal and the particular in moral judgment cannot be considered here except insofar as it bears on the Radical of Historical Representation—but there, it seems to me, the claim for the particularity of moral judgment is compelling. The instances of historical representation judged in that formula are individual events; no less necessarily, the weights attached to them would reflect the same particularity.

That there is no algorithm by which to determine the weight assigned to every possible event indicates that the determination here must be contextual. And the context most directly pertinent to its formation is provided, it seems to me, by the notion of a moral community—the interwoven dependencies and claims that, ill-defined as their boundaries are, are nonetheless distinguishable from the conception, indeed from the possibility, of a universal moral language, on the one hand, or a private moral language, on the other. The vagaries and so the dangers in relying on this contextual ground are evident, but they are no larger than what is entailed by their alternatives.

I offer two examples of the point indicated here. In the question period after a lecture that Saul Friedländer delivered in the fall of 1989 at a conference at Northwestern University titled "Lessons and Legacies [of the Holocaust]," the first question directed to Friedländer came from Arthur Butz, a faculty member at Northwestern. Since the lecture itself was not restricted to conference registrants, Butz had the right to be present; in the order of the meeting, he also had a right to be recognized by the chair and to question the speaker. What he did not have a right to—or obversely, what the speaker was not obligated to provide—was a response to his question, even to the relatively straightforward one that he asked. And in deciding not to respond to the author of *The Hoax of the Twentieth Century*—consciously overriding the academy's commitment to open discussion—Friedländer was, it seems to me, asserting a twofold limit: first, on the moral possibilities of historical representation, and second, on the extent of the moral community that is itself a part of that representation and from which, on this matter at least, Friedländer judged Butz to have separated himself. (I should note that this is my gloss on the exchange, not Friedländer's.)

Obviously, each of the two elements of this limit involves the risk of a slippery slope, and even to take the one step that Friedländer did involves a risk. But Friedländer's refusal to respond to Butz implicitly claimed a still larger risk and challenge on the other side—in the assumptions that "questions" are detachable from those who raise them, that questioners are themselves separable from the contexts in which they speak, and most fundamentally, that historical representations have no intrinsic moral standing. It seems to me that all three of these claims are rightfully disputed, not *uniquely* in their bearing on accounts of the "Final Solution" but certainly and markedly there, a crux that itself then becomes a ground for the representation of limits.

A second example appears in a statement published by a group of thirty-four French historians in *Le Monde* on 21 February 1979 against the background of a then recently published denial of the existence of gas chambers in the Nazi death camps (and so also a denial of the Holocaust):

> Everyone is free to interpret a phenomenon like the Hitlerian genocide according to his philosophy. . . . Everyone is free to apply to it one or another means of explication; everyone is free, up to the limit, to imagine or dream that these monstrous facts did not take place. They unfortunately did take place, and no one can deny their existence without outrage to the truth. . . . This is the obligatory starting point of any historical inquiry on the subject. . . . It is impossible to have a debate on the existence of the gas chambers. (My translation)

It is clear that the limit thus asserted is not drawn around anything like a "simple" matter of fact; on that basis, to deny the existence of the gas chambers would be no more excluded from discussion or representation than any other denial. What is asserted, I take it, is a moral *presence* for matters of fact, and thus a quite different account of what matters of fact, here or elsewhere, are.

Again, the menace of the slippery slope threatens; it is necessary to defend even this one step, given the frequency with which piety finds itself turned into moralism. It is not unreasonable, at any rate, to ask at a theoretical level whether a claim of the sort made by the French historians is or could ever be legitimate. For analysis that takes as a premise what has come to be known as the Naturalistic Fallacy, with the sharp line drawn there between fact and value, the answer to this question would obviously be no: facts immaculately conceived can only be immaculately judged. But if one rejects that premise—on the grounds that the moral weight of a fact may be as much an ingredient in it as any other of its features—then not only is it possible that limits like the one asserted by the thirty-four historians should be sustained but for some cases it would be implausible, even contradictory, not to. One could imagine here the inversion of a Kafkaesque tale in which the existence of a limit was proclaimed but what it "limited" or excluded was left unstated. The antihero of the tale is troubled, even obsessed by this absence. He grows old, beset by profligacy and angst in equal measures; try as he will, even his largest excesses fail to bring him into contact with the limit, to disclose what it is. He has not, he feels at the end, led a *full* life.

The claim that such representations of limits are warranted in general does not justify any *particular* limit; the indistinctness of practical in contrast to theoretical judgment applies here as well, for worse as well as for better. But here also the Radical of Historical Representation provides the basis for a useful distinction—even if, as it bears on the issue of the "Final Solution," it holds up a telescope to view something plainly in sight.

Art within the Limits of History

I referred earlier to a statement by Leonardo da Vinci concerned with artistic or pictorial rather than historical representation, and I would now complete the circle begun with that reference. For Leonardo, the "walls stained with damp, or . . . stones of uneven color" were accidental, incentives to the power of invention, which once evoked could then proceed on its own. Insofar as limits of representation were to appear in that context at all, then, they would be limits of the artist's imagination, not constraints imposed by the walls or stones. That what the artist "saw" could only equivocally be said to be representations of the walls or stones would be outweighed, one infers, by the limitlessness of the possibilities open to representation: anything imaginable could be represented here, with the walls and stones only occasions or causes not themselves sustained or evident representationally.

This ideal of artistic representation as boundless in principle recurs in post-Renaissance conceptions of art and aesthetics—at an extreme in romantic accounts of genius and originality but persistent also in less dramatic formulations that in other respects oppose the romantic emphasis on individualism. So, for example, Salman Rushdie, although himself confronted by unusually harsh claims for the limits of representation, reiterates even then his opposing view of literature as, by its nature, "the one place in any society where . . . we can hear the voices talk about everything in every possible way."[11]

It should be evident that all justification of censorship is separable from the question of whether limits of artistic representation are re-

---

11. Salman Rushdie, "Is Nothing Sacred?" *Granta*, no. 31 (1990): 97–111.

lated to limits of historical representation in the way I have been proposing. For again, the issue is not one of intrinsic or necessary boundaries, since for the imagination to formulate a limit—to imagine what could not be imagined—would already be to exceed it. The question, then, is not, in the relationship between the actual and the possible, what can or cannot be imagined, but whether limits apply to the forms that imagined representations do take in point of fact, or ought to take in point of value.

In this connection, imaginative writing about the "Final Solution" shares certain constraints with imaginative accounts of any historical subject. Where history figures in artistic representation, the details of historical chronicle have an importance that is absent or much reduced in representations in which specific historical events have no part. Admittedly, the line between what is and what is not fiction—in this instance, what is known as "Holocaust writing"—itself remains unclear. So, for example, in Saul Bellow's *Mr. Sammler's Planet*, Sammler, the reader learns piecemeal, had fought as a partisan in the European destruction; but this literary fact is quite off-center from the primary representation of the novel, set in the turmoil and uncertainty of New York middle-class and intellectual life in the late 1960s. Or in a more distinctive (because less serious) example, several pages in R. D. Rosen's mystery novel *Strike Three You're Dead* depict an encounter between the detective-hero and a tailor who is a concentration camp survivor, where this fact about the latter's biography, although given in some detail, is quite unrelated to the book's plot. The encounter thus amounts to a citation rather than a representation of the "Final Solution," and even if its use as a citation has some representational significance, that significance is clearly subordinate to other elements of the book.

There is, to be sure, a familiar and general problem for aesthetics: how an artistic or literary work's representation—what it is "about"—is to be determined. But that specific judgments of this matter may be disputed does not mean that the problem is irresolvable at a theoretical level or in other applications. For many texts that refer to the "Final Solution," the most pressing issue is not to determine whether that event is their subject but to assess its "representation-as" their subject—for one thing, in its relation to the limits that that subject brings with it. So far as such limits pertain, this compounds the burden already imposed by historical representation itself, with the dangers now coming from both sources rather than only the one.

The effect of this compounding of limits is noticeable even at the first—"chronicled"—levels of literary and historical fact. The writer may imagine, as George Steiner does in *The Portage to San Cristobal of A.H.*, that Hitler survived the war, later to emerge from hiding in South America; or, as Philip Roth does in *The Ghost Writer*, that Anne Frank, having "in fact" escaped Bergen-Belsen, then reappears as an aspiring young writer in wintry New England. But these imagined representations depend for their force on straightforwardly historical premises that the texts assume are known to the reader, namely, that the imagined possibilities so represented are at once fictional and false; that is, that they might in principle have been the case but in fact were not.

In this way, the limits of historical representation—*a fortiori* for representation beyond the level of chronicle—apply also to historical fiction, with the added burden now, however, of taking into account what is entailed in designedly figurative or trop-ic representation. About this, only a few rudimentary words. Whatever else they do, figurative discourse and the elaboration of figurative space obtrude the author's voice and a range of imaginative turns and decisions on the literary subject, irrespective of that subject's character and irrespective of—indeed defying—the "facts" of that subject, which might otherwise have spoken for themselves and which, at the very least, do not depend on the author's voice for their existence or structure. The claim is entailed in imaginative representation that the facts *do not* speak for themselves, that figurative condensation and displacement and the authorial presence they articulate will turn or supplement the historical subject, whatever it is, in a way that represents the subject more compellingly or effectively—in the end, more truly—than would be the case without them.

It seems to me crucial to recognize that certain possible subjects of artistic representation challenge this premise and that imaginative representations of the "Final Solution" are such an instance—not in the sense that the challenge is insuperable but in the sense that it is unavoidable, occurring both with unusual force and in an unusual form.

The Limits of Representation

The moral enormity based on the twofold denial of individuality and personhood in the act of genocide and the abstract bureaucracy that empowered the "Final Solution," moved by a corporate will and blindness to evil—these constitute a subject that in its elements is at odds with the humanizing effects of figurative discourse and the individuation of character and motivation that literary "making" projects onto its subjects. With this, a risk is added to the already severe one chanced in the assertions of even the most circumscribed historical representation, a risk that would hold even for subjects less heavily weighted morally than the "Final Solution" but that substantially increases the likelihood of *mis*representation, a danger manifested in moral as well as in cognitive terms.

Adorno's assertion of the barbarism—not the impossibility, but the barbarism—of writing lyric poetry after Auschwitz (*a fortiori* about Auschwitz)—is an instance of the application of this representational limit and one that at least in its premises ought to be taken seriously in any judgment of imaginative writing about the "Final Solution." Admittedly, even if Adorno's claim were accepted at face value (he himself subsequently qualified it),[12] a justification might be given in favor of the barbarism he warns against as a defense against still greater barbarism—against Holocaust denial, for example, or against forgetfulness. On this basis it could be held that even certain *mis*representations of the "Final Solution"—representations that seek the effects of melodrama or sentimentality or prurience—may nonetheless be warranted; even this writing, it could be (and has been) maintained, serves a purpose in calling attention to the historical occurrence itself, arguably doing this more effectively for some readers than other representations from which these failings are absent. In this sense, an unusual plea, based on an unusual subject, could also be entered for admittedly barbaric—"bad" or "false"—writing.

Not even this justification, however, would override what seems to me the most general limit of representation, the limit against which all

---

12. Theodor W. Adorno, "Engagement," in *Gesammelte Schriften* (Frankfurt am Main: Suhrkamp, 1974), 422; idem, *Negative Dialectics*, trans. E. B. Ashton (New York: Seabury, 1973), 362.

representation, and all other representational limits, must in the end be measured and which applies to writing about the "Final Solution" only more obviously but no more essentially than it does to writing about other subjects. This is the limit, and thus the alternative, of silence—and I do not mean here a silence intended to express the impossibility, the intrinsic inadequacy, of representation of the "Final Solution" (as suggested at various times by such different writers as George Steiner and Elie Wiesel). Substantial evidence, both theoretical and factual, argues against this claim—as substantial, at all events, as the evidence against claims for the unintelligibility of evil in any of its appearances. I mean rather a silence that emerges as a limit precisely because of the possibility of representation and the risks that that possibility entails. In these terms, silence is a limit for every individual representation or image, establishing the barrier of a simple but universal test. This is the question of whether, in comparison with the voice heard in the representation being considered, silence itself would have been more accurate or truthful or morally responsive. Could there be a more severe or more fundamental limit than this? And would it not apply, if it ever applied, to representations of the "Final Solution"?

4 | The Facts of Fiction

Three Case Studies in Holocaust Writing

Reflexive or self-referential questions are a constant source of embarrassment for philosophers and other theorists—none of them known for being easily embarrassed. So I set out from one such question gingerly, hoping to leave it quickly behind, although it needs to be stated in order to introduce the case studies I propose to discuss here. This question bears on the common distinction between fiction and nonfiction, with the "reflexive" part of the question asking whether the distinction itself is fiction or nonfiction. That is, which is it? More is at stake here than a quibble or a carp. For if the distinction between fiction and nonfiction were a fiction, we could as easily substitute its contradictory, simply eliminating the distinction; surely a fictional world would allow us this freedom. But if the distinction is nonfictional— that is, a fact, then the most to be claimed is that it results from circular reasoning or begging the question since it hopes to establish the distinction by assuming it.

Of course we might seek refuge in a compromise: the invitingly sensible position that views the divide between fiction and nonfiction as a convention or merely practical measure, adopted to solve such unruly problems as how to shelve the books in libraries or what universities can do to avoid being submerged under a single and mammoth Department of Literature that would include history and psychology as well as poetry. But this practical rationale brings with it the worst of both worlds, at once begging the question and still lacking any principled reason for the fiction/nonfiction distinction. We might just as "conventionally" arrange books in a library by the colors of their covers or divide university departments by the astrological signs of their faculty.

What, then, should we make of the supposed difference between fiction and nonfiction, that is, after we also reject the formula—pressed into service in the past for everything from beauty to obscenity—in which we first admit that we cannot say much about a given subject but then insist that we certainly know it when we see it. One solution, recently in fashion, would be simply to accept the deconstruction of the distinction, in effect eliding fiction and nonfiction, placing them on a single continuum with only certain accidental, never qualitative markers dividing them. On this continuum the writing of history becomes only another narrative form, distinguishable from the dreamwork or the novel or the long or short story only by the particular tale it tells, not by its kind.

It seems clear to me, however, that the history of the Holocaust—in fact and in writing—should have demonstrated once and for all the limitations of this conception of historical discourse. If history were only another manner of speaking (or writing), one trope or metatrope among others, there would be no basis for choosing (except as a matter of taste) between any one historical account and its contradictory. And then the hard fact of a particular genocide, the Nazi genocide or any other, would unavoidably lose whatever edge is claimed for it over its denial. Furthermore, not only the historiography of the Holocaust has pressed this case for a foundationalist, even a positivist view of truth—uncomfortably compelling even for critics who balk at its apparent simple- or single-mindedness. For we find this same pressure also present, and also constant, in the "imaginative" writing of the Holocaust, with repeated avowals there as well of historical and not only poetic or aesthetic authenticity. So, for a random clutch of examples: Thomas Kenneally's claim of veracity in his account of *Schindler's*

List, a claim that on the internal evidence of his novel alone could not possibly be true; Jean-Francois Steiner's similar assertion and then *his* imagined account of life in *Treblinka;* Art Spiegelman's dispute with the *New York Times Book Review* when it classified *Maus* on its "best-seller" list as fiction and the *Review*'s eventual concession, which moved the book one graph over, onto the "nonfiction" list, a change denied to Kenneally when he made the same plea for his book. And we have just recently heard the insistence of Elie Wiesel's literary agent, Georges Borchardt—evidently speaking for Wiesel himself—that *Night,* for so many years comfortably accommodated in the Library of Congress under the heading of fiction, really should be classified (or reclassified) as nonfiction, that is, I suppose, as memoir or autobiography. Walter Pater famously characterized art as "aspiring to the condition of music"; we can, I think, reasonably generalize that Holocaust fiction—imaginative writing about the Holocaust—typically if not invariably aspires to the condition of *history.*

And for good reason: What should we expect to be preeminent in a Holocaust novel or poem or drama? that which is novel or poetic or dramatic in the writing—or the Holocaust itself? Yet an uneasiness about this obvious disproportion has emanated from the side of art, specifically in the modern conception of art as a source of truth-telling, not only in its own aesthetic terms (there's nothing distinctively modern about that) but also as usurping or outstripping other competing and in any event more prosaic forms of truth. I don't mean to suggest that the grounds for the distinction between historical and imaginative discourse are easily discerned or articulated. I would argue, however, that the source of pressure in and around Holocaust writing in support of that distinction is also a source of evidence for it; in other words, that the fiction/nonfiction distinction is neither fiction nor question-begging fact nor merely social convention. Rather, that the distinction should be viewed not in aesthetic or cognitive terms at all (at least not initially) but as based on a moral foundation; furthermore, that the history of Holocaust writing and criticism provides strong evidence for this claim. Or, to put this last point differently: to deny or ignore the moral basis of the fiction/nonfiction distinction would leave the history of Holocaust writing and Holocaust criticism inexplicable.

To support this thesis, I present three brief accounts, or case histories, of Holocaust writing. Two will undoubtedly be familiar; the third, I have reason to believe, appears here for the first time.

Case Study 1

In 1993 the Australian Vogel Award for a first novel was given on the basis of its unpublished manuscript to *The Hand That Signed the Paper*, by Helen Demidenko, a twenty-two-year-old Australian writer; the terms of the award included publication of the novel by Allen and Unwin, and the novel, once published, went on to win two additional significant Australian literary prizes. In an author's note prefacing the novel, Demidenko wrote, "What follows is a work of fiction. . . . Nonetheless, it would be ridiculous to pretend that this book is unhistorical." Fair warning, one might say, although hardly a portent of either the aura surrounding the publication of the novel and its prizewinning career or what then began to emerge. In her personal statements, outside the novel, Demidenko claimed a Ukrainian father (Marko) who had emigrated to Australia in 1951 and then married her mother, another new arrival in Australia, from Ireland. At the time of her novel's publication (and for several years beforehand) the author emphasized the Ukrainian side of her heritage, sometimes to the point of wearing Ukrainian national dress; the novel itself (which, as the reader had been instructed, was "not unhistorical") is in effect a narrative of Ukrainian history during the Holocaust. Specifically, it relates the story of the Ukrainian father and uncle of the young woman protagonist, the father having participated in the Babi Yar massacre, the uncle having served as a guard at Treblinka, the two of them driven to those extremes by the great famine in the Ukraine for which Stalin and the Bolsheviks, predominantly Jewish in the novel's account, were responsible. The Holocaust—Babi Yar, Treblinka—thus emerges as part of an ongoing circle of atrocity and revenge, with the only way out of that circle (in the novel's own search for an ending) an embrace of contrition and forgiveness on all sides, a latter-day version of the deus ex machina. The novel's antisemitic characterizations were initially either overlooked or ignored by readers and critics, probably in deference to the unusual voice of the "implied author" and the still more unusual history claimed by the actual author. Under scrutiny, however, the latter history began to unravel, itself assuming a place in the author's fictional world. Her parents, it turned out, were neither Ukrainian nor Irish; rather, both were English immigrants to Australia. Their family name (and hers) was Darville. The name Demidenko, which she had adopted qua author (and which appeared in an early draft of her novel as the family name of its main characters), was not entirely a fiction: it was the name of a Ukrainian killer in the Holocaust known from the historical literature.[1]

Nothing in this series of disclosures as they trickled out, however, altered anything in the novel itself (except for the author's preface recounting her Ukrainian roots, which was omitted when the novel was reissued, when the author was listed as Helen Darville). The prize-awarding juries and her publishers were understandably embarrassed at having failed to notice how far their author's fictional world extended but not (at least not publicly) by the fiction of the novel as writing; some of them argued, in fact, that the artistic claims of the novel (and the author) were strengthened by the new disclosures since now the novel was revealed as still more demonstrably a work of the imagination.

This should, one supposes, have been the end of the matter, but of course it was not. The charges of fraud multiplied notwithstanding the oddity of their criticism, which objected to the novel's fiction as itself a fiction. And so the question I would pose in returning to the thesis initially posed: Why all the fuss? For if nothing substantive was altered in the novel as a result of the author's disclosures, and if the embarrassment of prize juries and publishers was a matter of their having acted in good faith but having been taken in by a true con artist—conned about *her* but not, as they persisted, about the novel—what difference does it make? Why such indignation about what turns out to be the fictional life of the author, when so many other authors (and nonauthors) also invent themselves as they go along? It wasn't the au-

1. For a fuller account of the "Demidenko" affair, see Anthony Daniels, "Literary Victimhood," *New Criterion*, September 1999, 4–9.

thor, after all, whom the publisher had published or for which the prizes were awarded. Anyone who buys a book because of its author's (supposed) biography, it might well be argued, can hardly fault the book if the author turns out to be somebody quite different. For what difference would or should that make anyway? (We recall the old saw about the authorship of the *Iliad* and the *Odyssey*, which, we learn, were written not by Homer but by somebody else with the same name.) More about this later.

Case Study 2

In 1995 another author's first book was published, in this case to immediate international acclaim. The author was a fifty-six-year-old musician and music teacher who lived in Switzerland but whose memoir—so the book claimed in its title—followed the contours of memory of a Jewish child born in Riga months before the outbreak of World War II and then almost immediately caught up by the Holocaust when it reached Latvia: separated from his family after the destruction of the Riga ghetto and deported (at the age of three or four) to Majdanek and then to a second camp, later named by him as Auschwitz. *Fragments*, the lead term in the book's title, accurately labeled the events recounted, which, even compared with other autobiographical accounts of horror with which many of its readers were acquainted, were indeed shattering: seeing other children driven by hunger to eat their own fingers, having his own head smashed against a wall by a camp guard, seeking out and standing in excrement for the sake of its warmth. To many readers it seemed that even if someone had set out to create extraordinary variations on the already extraordinary themes of suffering known from the Holocaust, it would be difficult to imagine, let alone to live through and survive, the "fragments" of Benjamin Wilkomirski's recollected wartime years (he would have been only six at the war's end). But this is in fact what, four years after the book's appearance, after the author's travels around the world and reception of awards made to the book in Paris, London, and New York, turns out to have been the case. That is, the "memoir" was indeed the fragments of imaginary memory, conjured by a non-Jewish Swiss native who had

The Facts of Fiction

been placed in an orphanage by his unwed mother and then adopted by a devoted Swiss Protestant couple whose name—Dössekker—he bore legally in Switzerland even at the time of his "memoir"'s publication. This "counterhistory" was uncovered and then described by a Swiss Jewish writer, Daniel Ganzfried, who traced the history of the author of *Fragments* by documents and interviews. Parts of this counterhistory still remain uncertain and perhaps will continue to remain so. Benjamin Wilkomirski (or Bruno Dössekker) has responded to the challenges to his book's authenticity on a number of occasions; various inconsistencies and vagaries have figured in those responses, and even their dominant common theme rehearses a cautious note that the author himself struck in an afterword to the original edition of the book, well before any external challenge had been voiced ("Legally accredited truth is one thing—the truth of a life is another"). In any event, the publishers of Wilkomirski's book have arrived at their own judgment: Schocken, the American publisher, has removed the book from the market; Suhrkamp, the original German-language publisher, first withdrew the hardcover edition and then completed the circle by withdrawing the paperback as well.[2]

What nobody has challenged in the now more than two-year-old controversy about the authenticity of the book's status as memoir is that its text remains unchanged by the questions raised about it. That is, in the literal sense of a text—the words on the printed page. One obvious solution, too blatant to be immediately acceptable, although almost certainly the book's fate in the long run, would be simply to reclassify it, changing its designation from nonfiction to fiction. If, as a number of prominent literary and Holocaust scholars agreed at the time of its first appearance, *Fragments* had unusual power as a text—according to one historian, it would "educate" even those already familiar with the Holocaust literature—then would not that power remain, quite apart from the actual biography of the author himself? So

2. See the accounts of Wilkomirski's "Memoirs" by Elena Lappin ("The Man with Two Heads," *Granta*, summer 1999, 7–65) and Philip Gourevitch ("The Memory Thief," *New Yorker*, 14 June 1999, 48–68).

indeed some critics and scholars have maintained: "The book is still powerful as a novel" has been asserted by a second historian of the Holocaust. A rather more skeptical literary critic recently taught the book in a class precisely in order to raise the question of what difference its status as fiction or nonfiction made. "My students," he reports, "said [that] if the book is good it[s factuality] doesn't matter." But is *that* a fact? Again, more about this later.

Case Study 3

I earlier suggested that I was confident that this third "case" would be presented here for the first time. It begins with the following text that has come into my possession by means that I am prepared to disclose later; the text itself has been unknown until now. The statement, dated and notarized on 7 April 1985, reads as follows:

To whom it may concern:

This statement is a confession. I write it in a time of great personal uncertainty, of ill health and stress; it may be that I shall yet withdraw or destroy this statement, although if it is being read, it will be clear that I did not do that. I have in any event stipulated that the person to whom I entrust the statement shall not release it until more than twelve years after my death. Why twelve? It is a good number. Released to whom? I leave that to my trustee, asking only that it be released outside my native land and on an obscure occasion. Why a confession? Because it is a statement of my own, written in my own hand and in my own words—in contrast to the many other words, *volumes,* that have appeared under my name, but that I now declare were not mine either to sign or to write. I will not attempt to explain why I lent my name in this fashion, except to say that I believed there was sufficient reason for doing so. Indeed there is only one matter that I wish to state and insist on here: that the writings which have appeared under my name were not in fact written by me—and that their true author swore me to secrecy concerning his identity except for one item: that never, during the period of the World War did he ever leave the boundaries of his native country—which was, I am free to say, also my own. That is, in fact, how we came to meet. It is true, as the public accounts have repeatedly stated, that I was held as a prisoner in a deportation camp; it is true that I was placed with other prisoners on a train that was bound for Auschwitz. But what happened after that has hitherto been unknown; it is not even interesting, at least for me, except for the fact that I managed, more by luck than by skill, to escape from the deportation train soon after it left the camp; the next two and a half years I spent in the northern mountains, in a small, remote village, cut off from the world. Although with some feelings of guilt, I remained there willingly, since it seemed to me that the world beyond that village did not bear thinking about, let alone inhabiting. Near the end of that time, a stranger appeared in the village—itself an extraordinary occurrence. What was more extraordinary were the stories he brought with him that he had begun to write on the basis of what he had heard, remarkable stories that he had imagined of someone who had lived through almost a year in the camp Auschwitz. Beyond the barbarism recounted in those stories, they included one striking oddity: the first person narrator who appeared in them laid claim to an earlier history that bore an uncanny resemblance to my own. The author, of course, knew nothing of this. He found a hut outside the village and continued to write there; he had, he told me, decided not to return to the world outside; what he was writing, he said, was at once his reason for leaving that world and for remaining anonymous: there was no longer any place in it, he insisted, for individual persons. It was then that I told him something of my own history, and of how his fictional narrator, that secret sharer, seemed to have lived my life in the years before the war. Out of this coincidence came the arrangement that continued until recently, when I learned of his death in the village. The details of how we managed to communicate with each other and with the publisher of his books, of how I returned to my professional and family life in my native city, how I contrived the appearance of authorship of writings that were not mine—all these are of no importance for this statement, not properly part of a confession at all. Do I feel remorse or regret for this deception? Some deceptions are too large for the person responsible for them to comprehend, let alone to judge; this one, after all, became my life. I, Primo Levi, attest to this.

Signed and notarized 7 April 1985, Turin

I trust that it will be obvious by this point why I am confident that readers come upon this account for the first time: in part because the statement is indeed published for the first time but more obviously because it was not Primo Levi who wrote it but me, and quite recently at that. It is, I grant you, an only too transparent fiction. But suppose for a moment that it were not—that I were able to show you convincing evidence that these *were* Levi's words; moreover, that what he asserts there could be independently verified by following his tracks to the village in which he spent the last year of the war instead of Auschwitz, and so on. What then of the collected works of Primo Levi—now to be designated the collected works of an anonymous author, unknown other than by the fact of his authorship, and now evidently all to be moved into the fiction sections of libraries and bookstores, together, one supposes, with *Sophie's Choice* and *The White Hotel?* The one-time Levi *oeuvre,* like the individual books in the two other (nonfictional) cases I have described, would remain unchanged in its words. But both books and words, and now also Primo Levi himself, are disclosed as having been imagined, not the faithfully deliberated accounts his readers have found in his work—his encounter with what otherwise appeared as an incomprehensible and terrible world—with his account leaving it no less terrible but certainly more comprehensible. Would that intelligibility, and his readers' commitment to him, still hold for the newly discovered, albeit anonymous author after this startling disclosure? The evidence, I believe, is to the contrary. The change *would* (and should) matter.

I CONCLUDE HERE quickly and abruptly, although there should properly be at least as much deliberation in drawing the moral of these case studies as in their telling. Two points in particular seem to me to apply to the three studies in common. First, the disquiet of which they have been the source—or in the case of Levi, would be—is not primarily due to the disclosure of deception. Nobody enjoys being tricked or taken in, least of all publicly, but it is, after all, a commonplace feature of everyday life. Of course such disclosures become more notable the larger the scale on which they are set; here also, as in the cases mentioned, comes the added piquancy of voyeurism and at times schadenfreude. But all this, I believe, has a much smaller part in the reaction evoked in these case studies than—and here the second point—the trust undone in them and by them on a subject that, because of its extraordinary moral weight, demands uncommon trust and the largest measure of authenticity in any representations or judgments based on it. It is there, in that moral weight, that the pressure for the fiction/nonfiction distinction originates, which also explains why fiction writers may at times pretend in their artfulness to be writing nonfiction, and why nonfiction writing is, and should be, zealous in guarding its borders. Is the subject of the Holocaust unique in making such demands? Hardly. Trust, after all, is part of the fabric of commonplace no less than of extraordinary events. Other recent "case studies," in settings of large if not equal dimensions to those of the Holocaust, might be cited, for example, the supposed autobiography of Rigoberta Menchu (*I, Rigoberta Menchu*, 1983),[3] who was later (in 1992) awarded the Nobel Peace Prize. Examination has shown that her book, which recounted a personal history of victimization and violation in Guatemala, could not have been *her* personal history. Is this important, her defenders have asked, since her alleged autobiography so credibly could have been hers (or someone else's)?

82

This returns us, in conclusion as in our beginning, to the question of the status of the distinction between fiction and nonfiction. The case studies presented seem to me to demonstrate that the line thus drawn is indeed a distinction *with* a difference. We may on occasion adopt it for merely practical reasons, but it matters, more basically, on moral grounds; that is, because of the character and the moral weight of its subjects. Otherwise, it would be arbitrary, a matter of chance, that the Holocaust has provoked such persistent arguments over the distinction between fiction and nonfiction. And the likelihood that these disagreements are chance occurrences is much slighter than that the distinction itself is probable.

---

3. Rigoberta Menchu, *I Rigoberta Menchu: An Indian Woman in Guatemala*, ed. and intro. Elisabeth Burgos-Debray, trans. Ann Wright (London: Verso, 1984); originally published as *Me llamo Rigoberta Menchu y asi menacio la concienza* (Mexico City: Siglo Veintiuno Editores, 1983).

The Importance of
Holocaust *Mis*representation   5

Metaphysics may be a mug's game, but those who think they can avoid it by burying their heads in the sand are likely to wind up playing the game anyway but from the other end (reviving Aristotle's *Posterior Analytics?*). This is, it seems to me, a lesson taught by the three essays in the *History and Theory* forum "Representing the Holocaust" by Hans Kellner, Wulf Kansteiner, and Robert Braun.[1] Those essays differ tactically and rhetorically, but a common enemy—realism in all its guises —motivates them, serving as the alien "other" against which their conclusions also stand in solidarity. It may appear on the face of it unlikely, even unseemly, that historians should set themselves against history in this way, against the idea of a ground in fact to which the historians' account must answer, the more so when the "fact" involved concerns that complex of events that has come to be titled the Holocaust.

But so it is, and as a view posed by serious historians about such a serious issue it too must be taken seriously, not least because a major

1. Hans Kellner, "'Never Again' Is Now"; Wulf Kansteiner, "From Exception to Exemplum: The New Approach to Nazism and the 'Final Solution,'"; and Robert Braun, "The Holocaust and Problems of Historical Representation," in *History and Theory* 33 (1994): 127–44, 145–71, and 172–97, respectively.

part of their challenge is indeed directed against the traditional view, as I have just summarized it, of what the writing of history is. That basically oppositional stance on their part may explain why the essays do not go on to consider, let alone to defend, their own views of historical representation, but obviously it does not justify that avoidance, which has the effect of undercutting their initial criticism as well. It is unlikely, for any two conceptual alternatives, that the choice favoring either of them will come without certain costs, and in this case there is also something more than that: the reluctance of the three authors to give an accounting of their own proposal is proportionate to the strength of the one they reject.

The topic of the forum itself, "Representing the Holocaust," has been much discussed, of course; and it was in fact the history of that discussion that motivated the three contributors. The principal question that emerges as an issue in this history can be simply formulated: Are there any special limitations or demands that the character of the Holocaust does or should impose on its historical representation? Or is the normal pattern of historical discourse itself so episodic and "constructed" that representations of even extreme events like the Holocaust require no special formulas or dispensations? This binary question—it is one question, after all, not two—evidently assumes a "normal," that is, *non*special, form of historical representation as a background against which specific representations (including those of the Holocaust) will be assessed. The question cited thus asks whether changes in the normal form are required by the unusual character of the Holocaust, either on a "one-off" basis or in the normal form as such. The three authors differ on certain aspects of what they take this normal form of historical representation to be, but they do not disagree in their conception of the defining feature of that form, namely, its mediated and contextualist and so also its antirealist basis. Nor do they disagree on their negative answer to the question of the Holocaust's special representational status. There are, in this common view, no special requirements or limitations in the historical representation of the Holocaust, certainly none that would alter the normal and thus generally applicable form of historical representation.

If the question of what the normal form of historical discourse is were put aside, the claim that there are no special limitations imposed by any subject would be controversial only in its exclusion of accounts of the Holocaust that assert its historical uniqueness or its historical "unrepresentability." Those two claims are by no means equivalent or mutually entailed (as Kansteiner assumes), but this objection is a small matter in the larger context. At least it would be a small matter if the rejection of the two claims themselves were based on historical grounds. Admittedly, some advocates of the Holocaust's uniqueness or unrepresentability have argued from theological or other transhistorical premises, and such claims can hardly be contested in historical terms. But there is also a historical question about the existence of precedents to the Holocaust (or to the phenomenon of genocide), as has been demonstrated in the assembling of evidence that Steven Katz undertook in support of his broadly based thesis that the convergence of causal factors in the Holocaust is historically unprecedented.[2] Whether or not one accepts Katz's assessment of the evidence, and whatever one infers from it if it is accepted, nothing in those conclusions would disable the historical question of whether there are precedents to the Holocaust or would prove that a denial of any such precedents is intrinsically mystifying or ideologically tendentious—which is how Kellner, Kansteiner, and Braun finally "represent" that view.

This objection on their part, however, would be only an eddy in the wider current of the three accounts of historical representation if the problematic status they ascribe to what I shall be calling here "historical facts" had been argued for rather than simply assumed.[3] But their nonhistorical dismissal of claims of the Holocaust's historical distinctiveness is symptomatic of their own more basic and still more trans-

2. Steven Katz, *The Holocaust in Historical Context* (New York: Oxford Univ. Press, 1994).

3. I would instance here—symptomatically—their misreading of my own work as maintaining the "uniqueness" and the "unrepresentable" or incomprehensible nature of the Holocaust, all of which are views I have opposed in *Act and Idea in the Nazi Genocide* (Chicago: Univ. of Chicago Press, 1990) and elsewhere (see, e.g., "The History of Evil and the Future of the Holocaust," in *Lessons and Legacies*, ed. Peter Hayes [Evanston: Northwestern Univ. Press, 1991], 90–105; "The Interpretation of Limits," in *Probing the Limits of Representation*, ed. Saul Friedländer [Cambridge: Harvard Univ. Press, 1992], 300–317; and "Genocide," in *Encyclopedia of Ethics*, ed. Lawrence Becker [New York: Garland, 1992], 760–61).

parently a priori premise concerning the normal form of historical representation: on the one hand, a rejection of all such representation as even possibly referential or factual; on the other hand—in the positive "moment" of their premise—the assertion of historical representation (with all history as representational) as uniformly contextual and interpretive: passed through a variety of filters and lenses to such an extent that there is no way of distinguishing the lens or filter from the objects and events seen through them.

86   Their other differences aside, the three authors' agreement on these two principles is firm and unquestioned. And it is on the basis of those principles that they then conclude that no exceptions need be made for representing the Holocaust. Indeed, why should there be exceptions, since one possible formulation of the view they are defending is that every event is an exception. At this poststructuralist stage on the mind's way, we are given to understand, only the naif, if not also the knave, would credit historical discourse with a "stable referent" (Kellner) or the possibility of "factual singularity" (Kansteiner) or the "'reality' of the past as an object of study" (Braun). Those mythic concepts, we learn, have been broken once and for all, and we see this common oppositional stance epitomized in Braun's use of quotation marks wherever he finds himself obliged to mention the term *fact* or *truth* (or *reality*). Like the skeptic's raised eyebrows, those quotation marks surround and mean to defeat any use of language that hints at an extralinguistic or extrainterpretive historical source or referent. Since no such extrainterpretive fulcrum exists, any historical claim of uniqueness must allow for another representation in which the object at issue is not exceptional but commonplace—a possibility that by itself defeats the original claim.

The point at issue here, again, is not the substantive question of the Holocaust's uniqueness—which seems to me largely, in arguments pro and con, a red herring—but the normal form prescribed by the symposiasts for historical analysis by their practice as well as in principle. Again, what they object to is in both these modalities clear: whatever is permitted historical representations of the Holocaust, it is not the reactionary invocation of nineteenth-century realism or positivism—as,

IMAGE AND FACT

for example, in Ranke's tropological and thus self-refuting view of history as the search for the *eigentlich*. Insofar as this proscription applies to the normal form of historical discourse in general, it holds also for historical representations of the Holocaust; harder justice in that case, perhaps, but justice nonetheless. And even if Kellner allows that some forms of discourse may be more "appropriate" than others for "some" events, that does not entail a point-zero, and indeed there is no such point, at which the structure of discourse is not itself part of the subject of discourse. The Hayden White of *Metahistory* is thus recalled nostalgically by all three authors; their erstwhile forebear, groundbreaker in the discovery of history as narrative form, has alas now regressed, evidently troubled by the phenomenon of the Holocaust in relation to his own earlier historiographic tour de force. Now he looks to the middle voice or, in any event, to *some* voice that might speak for non-interpreted facts, that is, for literary or political counterrevolution. And not only shouldn't this be done, according to the three symposiasts, it can't be.

What arguments are made for this dismissal of historical realism? One might dispute this question itself on the grounds that where the status of facts or truth is at issue, it begs the question to require refutations in their traditional form. To be sure, the latter consideration doesn't prevent certain voluntary inconsistencies. ("The most elementary fact about the modern historical profession is that it produces an enormous amount of discourse," writes Kellner [141]. What silent miracle, we ask, keeps the subject of that sentence—"the most elementary fact"—afloat?) In general, however, the oppositional point of departure in the three essays carries over into their positive moment, shaping their respective versions of an adequate, or at least more adequate, view of historical representation, although still without adducing evidence or proof. (Kansteiner claims only to be identifying the "limits and blind spots" in each of the two paradigms he describes, but he leaves no doubt which of them is in his view the blinder of the two, perhaps more than metaphorically associating it with its older age.) And again, like the negative critique in the three essays' origins, the refrain here is constant.

Kellner: The rhetorical constitution of events depends for its existence on the social codes that prevail in a group, a time, a place. (140)

Kansteiner: Only *Alltagsgeschichte* . . . offers the kind of consistent, intuitively [!] convincing image of Nazism which furthers historicization proper, that is the routinization of the representation of Nazism compatible with the parameters of historiography and of more popular forms of historical culture. (171)

Braun: In our perception of past social reality vis-à-vis documents and other "facts," there is no difference between the politically possible, the socially plausible, and the morally imaginary—nor do we know with which we are dealing. (196)

To be sure, some room is left at the edges of these assertions. Kellner's reference to "the *rhetorical* constitution of events" leaves open the possibility of another means of constituting them; Kansteiner concedes a potential "problem inherent in structuralist poetics" (as in James Young's *Writing and Rewriting the Holocaust*), insofar as that theory provides no grounds for dismissing "certain appropriations of the Holocaust" in favor of others (159); Braun, in claiming the legitimization of all accounts of the past "by the authority of the present," acknowledges the latter as at least a provisional terminus, although since the present is constantly being superseded by another present, it would be difficult to find much consolation (or historical stability) in this. And indeed, for the others as well, what is given with the one hand is invariably taken back directly. The three agree that the locus of history is always and only a point at the convergence of vectors of social custom or political power or linguistic figuration or moral tendentiousness. Not only do facts never speak for themselves but, post-Kantians all, have we not suffered enough from political and literary and historical mystification to recognize in the language of facts or referentiality only another appeal to the long discredited image of "things-in-themselves"? Are we now to reintroduce them in the guise of "facts-in-themselves"? The alternative is clear and ready; indeed, we can take not only comfort but pleasure in the "irredeemably earthly and immanent status of interpretation" (Kellner, 144), in the fact that "after Auschwitz poetry can be written, but history, as the 'realistic' interpretation of the past, cannot" (Braun, 196).

And here occurs the metaphysical failure of nerve that at once disables the symposiasts' criticism of the normal form of historical representation as linked to referentiality and the normal, "constructivist" version by which they mean to replace it. At the most immediate level, this failure becomes apparent from the analysis of ordinary usage: if representation or interpretation is—grammatically—the representation or interpretation of some "thing," what is the ontological status of whatever the representation or interpretation is *of?* Or more explicitly, in rehearsing what had been the forum's ostensive title, "Representing the *What?*" No one would deny that the term *Holocaust* is a matter of (disputed) convention as a term, and no one would deny that certain of the referents that the title *Holocaust* putatively designates may vary from account to account. But it is still clearer and more certain that other core elements are common to *any* account of the Holocaust (including, perversely enough, those that deny its occurrence) and that these core elements are constant not as a matter of convention but as a matter of—dare we say it?—fact.

Kellner objects to the proposal in an essay of mine (chapter 3 above) in which I claim that historical chronicles are extraterritorial, that is, noninterpretive: "But this," he announces, "is mistaken. A chronicle is the result of a pre-existing narrative; it is not the origin of such a narrative" (138). There are two alternative positions that Kellner might be disputing here. The first of these would construe a chronicle as a corporate structure of selected, albeit elementary, data. To call such a chronicle mimetic or directly referential would of course be "mistaken": the act of selection precludes such claims. Who would deny that chronicles are in this sense narrative-dependent?

There *is* an issue, however, in the question of whether the items constituting a chronicle (that is, its atomic elements, or more prosaically, the facts: who did what to whom, when, or where) are individually dependent—ontologically, epistemically—on a "pre-existing" narrative. And that indeed is the issue I reiterate here against the three contextualist views of historical representation in the forum as they would place the Holocaust or any other historical event (that is, "event") always and entirely within the circle of interpretation. If the narrative-dependence of facts holds in general, then for any particular narrative and its derivative "facts" an alternative "pre-existing" narrative might produce other, very possibly contradictory "facts." Narrative and interpretation first, in other words; facts, second. The implication here is, or should be, clear: if the claim is not asserting tautologically that finite narratives and chronicles are finite (in this context, selective), then it will be advocating this second line of argument and the "normal" form of historical representation it presupposes. Not only is history accessible only in variant, sometimes conflicting narratives but nothing that the narratives tell or talk about is exempt. We must distrust the tale as well as the teller—with no place else to turn.

That the Holocaust has at times been proposed as a test case for historical representation is due, of course, to its moral enormity. And so far as the normal form of historical representation in general is concerned, the judgment about that test case by the authors of "Representing the Holocaust," to the effect that the Holocaust changes nothing in this normal form, may well hold. But one could accept that claim and still maintain that the Holocaust is a test case of the normal form itself. And so indeed I would argue, not for its uniqueness as a test case but because the consequences that hinge on it (which the contributors to the forum are consistently willing to ignore) demonstrate so graphically what is at stake in the issue of representation.

Consider this item of chronicle: "On January 20, 1942, Nazi officials at Wannsee formulated a protocol for the 'Final Solution of the Jewish Question.'" There are, to be sure, matters that require further specification in this statement, for example, the identity or status of the Nazi officials or an answer to the question of exactly when the substance of the Wannsee protocol was composed. But with or without such additional clauses, the crucial question remains whether what the statement asserts, and so its truth or falsity, is essentially a matter of interpretation. Is the statement's truth or falsity a function only of a larger narrative and thus open to contradiction on any or every point when transposed to another narrative?

There is a large, obvious, and, in the matter of both Holocaust studies and truth, decisive difference between answering yes and answering no to these two questions. So far as concerns everything they affirm and nothing they deny, Kellner, Kansteiner, and Braun seem committed to answering yes to both questions. And insofar as the logic of their view dictates that response, it also entails that an alternative narrative to the one they presumably accept, which would affirm the occurrence of the Wannsee Conference on the date stated, could with equal conviction and force find it *not* to have occurred, then or perhaps ever. Such a contradiction between two "historical" conclusions would be a function of the different narrative structures from which they emerge. And although one of those narratives might be more to a given reader's taste than the other, it would indeed be taste and not anything else, nothing as crude or brute as "facts," that would decide between them. For about narratives, too, *non disputandum est.* Is this indeed what they, and the several variations of contextualism they respectively propose, mean to affirm? If not, on what grounds do they deny it? That is, on what grounds that they have otherwise not ruled out?

The issue here is perilously either/or. *Either* there is a point-zero of historical writing, an element of reference—facts. *Or* history is as you like it, not only in the stratosphere where historians and readers on almost every account enjoy something in the way of free and imaginative flight but also, well before that, in the trenches where the masses of names, dates, and numbers elbow one another for place. Can any possible narrative serve as the superstructure for any sub- or infrastructure of fact? that is, as capable of reversing or redoing any or all of the latter's elements? In the many historical accounts that have been given of it, the Holocaust has been described with a variety of (sometimes conflicting) emphases and from different perspectives. How could anything else be expected from the meeting of a complex and large mass of data and a "group" of historians who differ as much from one another *as* historians as the group as a whole does from others. But to say that historical narratives when they go beyond the items of chronicle are unfettered by anything more than the historian's will or imagination is to imply that the items of chronicle are also functions of will or imagination—thus, in the example cited, that it is the *historian's* responsibility to decide whether Nazi officialdom did or did not meet at Wannsee at all. Most people—including, I would guess, historians themselves—would be reluctant to say that whether or not they existed five minutes ago depends on what historians, singly or collectively, say about that question. Almost as reluctant as they would be to have historians decide whether they will continue to exist five minutes from now. And the basis for this resistance would not be a matter of psychology or physics or linguistic tropology, which is how, in various combinations reflecting *their* imaginations and will, Kellner, Kansteiner, and Braun represent the writing of history. Does anyone really believe, or act as if he believed, that whether the Holocaust occurred or not depends on what the historians say about that question? It is in this sense that the possibility of *mis*representing the Holocaust is a condition of representing it—with both of these dependent on a referent that is more than only a representation.

Eye and Mind | II

Reflecting the Holocaust

The Arts of History | 6

Hilberg on Hilberg: The Man and the Book

Autobiographies typically encompass a life, detailing whatever follows the author's beginning up to the time of writing. This is not entirely the writer's story, of course, since he relies on others for news of his earliest days, and he does not come even that close to reporting his death. Something like completeness is possible, however, as autobiographers base their narratives on certain "defining" themes or moments; even without these, autobiographies still purport to tell everything worth telling. By contrast, memoirs restrict themselves to "slices" of a life—the terms of a presidency, the landmarks of a voyage—with the boundaries around them varied but always present and always with a space separating the memories recorded from the life as a whole.

Like many distinctions, such differences between autobiography and memoir are most intriguing at their intersection, which is where we find Raul Hilberg's *The Politics of Memory*.[1] For this slim volume has

1. Raul Hilberg, *The Politics of Memory: The Journey of a Holocaust Historian* (Chicago: Ivan R. Dee, 1996).

the extent of an autobiography, as Hilberg refers to his birth in Vienna (in 1926) and then details his subsequent journey from a vantage point sixty-five years later, provoked then to reflect backward by an occasion he declares to be "the end": the silent reception of his just-published book, *Victims Perpetrators Bystanders* (1992). In substance, however, *The Politics of Memory* is a memoir: the slice of a life defined by Hilberg's role as the once and future author of *The Destruction of the European Jews* (henceforth, *Destruction*). Virtually everything Hilberg recalls in his book as occurring before or after the 1961 publication of *Destruction* is cued by that event. In this sense, the career of that one book *is* Hilberg's life; memoir thus becomes autobiography. And this, despite the efforts Hilberg makes to divert the reader of this more formal memoir/autobiography to his other works—urging the originality of *Victims Perpetrators Bystanders* or insisting on the importance for social history of the diary of Adam Czerniakow, chairman of the Warsaw *Judenrat* (Jewish Council), which he coedited (1979).

It becomes quickly evident, however, that Hilberg himself has no more chance of shaking free of *Destruction* than does the field of Holocaust studies more generally, which continues to owe more to that one book than to any other. Substantial studies of the Holocaust or its background appeared before *Destruction* (for example, by Leon Poliakov and Gerald Reitlinger), and many important works have appeared since. But the categories that Hilberg first articulated—of the personae of the drama, the "victims, perpetrators, bystanders"; of the stages of the genocide, "identification, expropriation, concentration, annihilation"; and then of the complex lines of command and obedience that he found to sustain the process—defined what have remained the basic angles of vision for historical writing about the Holocaust. These were, furthermore, grounded by Hilberg in an extraordinary mass of detail that reconstructed the mechanism of the "destruction," a matching of idea and instrumentality unrivaled in Holocaust or, indeed, much other historiography. Hilberg describes in his memoir/autobiography his childhood fascination with trains, hardly an unusual passion for a young boy at that time. Much more unusual was the adult Hilberg, who found in the rail system organized by the Nazis the low-tech but high-efficiency means on which the "Final Solution" depended. Looking backward from the production lines of death in the camps, he first imagined and then located the train schedules, the orders, the personnel, and the economic arrangements required for the system of transport required to supply them. Has any moment in the innumerable Holocaust testimonies been more stark or chilling than Hilberg's summary of the German Railway's price schedule announcing to the S.S. what the charges would be for transporting "passengers" to the camps in the East? "The basic charge was the third-class fare: 4 pfennig per track kilometer. Children under 10 were transported for half this amount; those under four went free. . . . For the deportees one-way fare was payable; for the guards a round-trip ticket had to be purchased" (*Destruction*, 411). 97

But again, *Destruction* is more than only a dramatic narrative, and indeed more than a pioneer work in a narrow field of historical study, however important. It is a masterpiece of historiography, extraordinary in its nuanced grasp of the *alltäglich* data of a complex bureaucracy and then in synthesizing those data into the arguably unprecedented general pattern of the "Final Solution." On a topic to which unusual energy and moral commitment, as well as considerable resources, have been given, Hilberg's book remains after thirty-five years and four editions a necessary work; its standards for historical analysis and its applications of them figure still in virtually all historical writing about the Holocaust, whether the writers working in its shadow like it or not.

Hilberg himself can hardly be unaware of his influence; he does not appear even in his own memoir/autobiography as a notably modest man. And notwithstanding the bleak Boston morning of discontent that, as he tells it, triggered the recollections gathered here—despair over his sense of public indifference to his work—he has been the recipient of numerous and substantial honors. Even readers appreciative of *Destruction*'s achievement, however, have at times expressed certain reservations about it, and it is on this part of the response to his work rather than on the esteem accorded it that Hilberg's recollections focus. That some criticism would be almost inevitable is obviously small consolation for him. (The duchess of Windsor revealed high society's secret that "you can never be too thin or too rich"; surely the academy's version of the secret would be that "you can never have too much praise.")

Readers of Hilberg's memoir/autobiography thus hear mainly about obstacles and criticism on the historian's journey. These were, to be sure, formidable, beginning with Hilberg's solitary venture, while a graduate student at Columbia and still financially dependent on his immigrant parents, into a field of scholarship that didn't exist. His struggle to tell the story of his painful topic, however, appears in Hilberg's recollection as almost the least of his problems, as he moves quickly past that to the obstacles he encountered afterward in seeking a wider audience for the expanded dissertation (i.e., *Destruction*). So he cites here a series of rejection letters from academic publishers—the presses at Columbia, where his dissertation had won a university prize, Princeton, and Oklahoma—as well as Yad Vashem. Finally, with the help of a stranger's unexpected subvention, Hilberg found a small and short-lived Chicago publisher, Quadrangle Books, which brought out *Destruction* in an edition notable mainly for its flimsy paper and double columns of printing.

The book's postpublication history afforded little respite. Corporate mergers sent *Destruction* on its own journey from Quadrangle to several other (unenthusiastic) houses until finally the third edition appeared in 1985 with Holmes and Meier, which still publishes it but which Hilberg, evidently piqued at its handling there, avoids naming. The fourth edition (1988) was published by Fayard in French translation with commercial success, and in 1990 S. Fisher Verlag published a paperback German edition, which also found a receptive audience. (The contrast between the book's neglect in the United States and its acceptance in Europe is a continuing grudge motif of Hilberg's.)

A less palpable specter, however, also shadows these material difficulties: the impress of *Destruction* on Hilberg himself and his difficulty in finding his way beyond it. Hilberg describes a notable parallel to this in the person of his principal mentor at Columbia, Franz Neumann, the author of *Behemoth: The Structure and Practice of National Socialism* (1942). Neumann anticipated both the significance of Hilberg's project and the resistance it was likely to encounter: "It's your funeral,"

Hilberg recalls Neumann's mordant blessing of his dissertation proposal. Neumann was in any event supportive, directing his one criticism—a criticism that would be repeated many times by others—at Hilberg's claim (which he then omitted in the dissertation but reinstated in the book) that in their response to the Nazi threat the Jews by a combination of compliance and self-deception "cooperated in their own destruction." Hilberg reports that Neumann accepted this assessment of the Jewish response but felt that it should not be said, although the comment by Neumann that Hilberg quotes as evidence— "This is too much to take"—would not by itself imply *agreement*.

Although Neumann continued to write and remained an influential teacher at Columbia, his *Behemoth,* which is still a standard reference, was unquestionably his major achievement. When he died suddenly in an automobile accident in 1954, Hilberg, then writing his dissertation while teaching in Puerto Rico, reflected on the contrast in Neumann's career before and after his great work appeared and asked himself, as he recalls it here: "What, after all, can a man do after he has written *Behemoth?*" Hilberg is reluctant, however, to recognize that same rhetorical question in relation to his own "Behemoth"; his wish to free himself from that book for later work is constantly overrun by the first book's echoes.

Thus, again, a large part of his memoir/autobiography reports on the critical aftermath of *Destruction.* One of this book's six sections, for example—two chapters, one of them titled "The Thirty-Year War" —is devoted to settling scores run up in the critical reception of *Destruction.* A notable instance of this involves three women (as it happens—or is it?) historians with whom Hilberg found himself professionally entangled. Hilberg does not take Nora Levin, Lucy Dawidowicz, or even Hannah Arendt seriously as either historians or thinkers, but they have, he finds, distorted his work or misrepresented their relationship to it in ways that he condemns in both scholarly and personal terms. Levin, Hilberg claims, used material from Hilberg's *Destruction* in her own book *The Holocaust* (1968) without acknowledgment. Dawidowicz in *The War against the Jews* (1975) mistakes crucial issues that Hilberg had already and more carefully worked out, in particular the matter of Nazi intentions leading up to the "Final Solution";

The Arts of History

and adding insult to error, she omits reference to Hilberg in her account of Holocaust historiography, *Historians and the Holocaust* (1982). Arendt, Hilberg later discovered, was the external reader for Princeton University Press who recommended rejecting *Destruction* as "not a sufficiently important contribution as a case-study in public administration to stand alone on that ground"; a scant four years later, in *Eichmann in Jerusalem,* Arendt acknowledged her own large debt to the by then published work.

Hilberg's fundamental quarrel with Arendt, however, is on substantive issues, and although even his statement of these conveys a sense of personal injury, in describing them Hilberg provides succinct formulations of questions that even now remain central to the historiography of the Holocaust. One of these, already mentioned, concerns the design of the "Final Solution" and Dawidowicz's suggestion that Hitler had planned the genocide of the Jews—*intended* it—as early as the 1920s, even in 1918. The questions of exactly what the Nazis intended, and when, and who was responsible for it—or more generally, what is meant by historical intention, individual or corporate—have been central issues in Holocaust historiography. It has been generally conceded that Dawidowicz's account is at best oversimplified both empirically and theoretically, and Hilberg's criticism of her position along these lines not only summarizes a compelling opposing view but also serves as an essential part of the architectonic of his own thinking. Hilberg's conception of the causal process of the "Final Solution" is, well, *historical;* that is, incremental, claiming not a one-time decision but a progressive response to circumstances that at each stage required further decisions and that only after a series of lesser steps culminated in genocide. "The decisions themselves were taken in steps. . . . There was an evolution in the procedure of decision-making . . . gradually laws gave way to decrees, and decrees to commitments, written orders, oral orders, and finally no orders. . . . The Germans did not know in 1933 what they were going to do in 1935. The ultimate goal of annihilation . . . was not even formulated until 1941" (64). Hilberg does not repeat in *The Politics of Memory* the complex argument on which he earlier based this conclusion, although he cites additional evidence that historians like Christopher Browning and Uwe Adam have since provided. But inasmuch as he is here writing about the writing of history rather than about history itself, he can hardly be faulted for this.

Two other important aspects of Hilberg's position in *Destruction* emerge from his account in his memoir/autobiography of his disagreements with Arendt in her *Eichmann in Jerusalem*. The first of these is his objection to Arendt's characterization of the "banality" of Nazi, at least of Eichmann's, evil. Although that thesis might have been expected to strike a responsive chord in Hilberg, who analyzed the layers of Nazi bureaucracy much more thoroughly than did Arendt, precisely the opposite is the case. The standard features associated with bureaucracy—its mindless repetition, hierarchies, and credo of "following orders," its *banality*—do not, in Hilberg's view, explain or account for the animus that sustained the "Final Solution." Eichmann's initiatives in finding "pathways" through the "thicket of the German administrative machine for his unprecedented actions" (150) were active and deliberate; furthermore, in the "Final Solution" as a whole, the "all-encompassing readiness [of the German people], which had to be deep-rooted, carried certain implications for the question of what Germany was all about," contradicting the "notion that the Nazis had imposed their will on an unwilling German population" as well as the common belief, even in the face of that genocide, "of the essential goodness of ordinary people the world over" (124–25). There exists, then, ample evidence of a will to murder expressing itself *through* the Nazi bureaucracy, a compelling malevolence that was not banal at all. That evidence seriously undermines Arendt's conclusion (as it also deflates Daniel Goldhagen's recent contention of the originality of his charge of German malevolence and widespread culpability).

In a second objection that Hilberg raises here against Arendt, he reacts against readers who elide his view with Arendt's charge of the collaborative role of the *Judenräte* in the ghettoes, a charge that at the time when *Eichmann in Jerusalem* appeared stirred more acrimony than her view of the banality of evil. Hilberg objects here to what he takes to be the superficiality of Arendt's claim: she did not go far enough. When she criticizes the *Judenräte* for cooperating with the Nazis—Arendt estimated, on what grounds she never says, that as many as half the Jews who were killed would have survived if not for this—she ignores what

Hilberg sees as the deeper connection between the *Judenräte* and the communities they represented. For it is there, according to Hilberg, in patterns of conduct ingrained in Jewish communities over centuries of life in Europe, that an explanation of the Jewish reliance on tactics of "alleviation" and "anticipatory compliance" with Nazi orders is to be found; the *Judenräte*, in other words, were only expressions or symptoms of something more deeply rooted. In the same vein, he reiterates, the "time-honored Jewish reaction to danger" accounted for the failure of the Jews to recognize the peculiar character of the Nazi threat and their inability to oppose it even when they did. In writing *Destruction*, he recalls, "I had to examine the Jewish tradition of trusting God, princes, laws, and contracts. Ultimately I had to ponder the Jewish calculation that the persecutor would not destroy what he could economically exploit. It was precisely this Jewish strategy that dictated accommodation and precluded resistance" (126–27).

This formulation by Hilberg makes clear that if his view of the Jewish response to the Nazi genocide has changed at all, it has only become harsher. Indeed he regards the multitude of critics of his interpretation as themselves providing confirmation of it (this obviously makes the argument a hard one for him to lose). As the Holocaust has been reconstructed in Jewish institutional memory—so Hilberg now analyzes his critics on this point—the Jews could be only victims or heroes, possibly both; the claim that they were themselves implicated in their fate would thus be not only repugnant but impossible. For Hilberg, such historical apologetics explain the criticism directed against him before Arendt's book appeared and still more harshly afterwards. An intimation of that criticism figured earlier in the letter of 24 August 1958 in which the director of Yad Vashem reported that institution's decision not to publish *Destruction*: "The Jewish historians here make reservations concerning the historical conclusions you draw, both in respect of the comparisons with former periods, and in respect of your appraisal of the Jewish resistance (active and passive) during the Nazi occupation" (110). For Hilberg, the explanation for this resistance is obvious: his conclusion was, as Franz Neumann had predicted, "too much to take."

And certainly Hilberg's position on this issue *is* hard to take. But is it only that? only "too much"? Or is there not also a genuine historical question underlying the reaction? Elsewhere in the present memoir, Hilberg describes the care he took with the language of *Destruction*. He did not, for example, use the term *murder* to describe the Nazis' actions (although he clearly believed it warranted) because it was "accusatory"; he would not employ "exculpatory" terms like *execution,* since this made the "victims into delinquents," nor *extermination,* since this "likened [the victims] to vermin" (87–88). Yet he does not even now consider that the connection he posits between the Jewish lack of overt resistance and their past history might warrant a subtler explanation than the "Jewish" factor he cites as a cause in his characterization of "Jewish strategy" or "Jewish calculation." Is it so obviously a *Jewish* calculation (and aside from that, so obviously unwarranted) to believe that even Nazis would act out of self-interest? (That the Nazis did not do so has been a finding drawn from the "Final Solution," not one that was evident or that seemed even likely beforehand.)

Hilberg's explanation of the Jewish response to the Nazi threat, which he reiterates in his memoir/autobiography—as well as his attack on those who have criticized him for it—leaps over centuries of culture and thousands of miles of geography more casually than he traverses days in detailing the events of the Holocaust. Perhaps any historical explanation (in contrast to description) can be similarly charged with underdetermination, but its weakness here is notable because Hilberg so rarely ventured other historical explanations in his earlier work. To be sure, his claim of the Jews' cooperation in their own destruction might in the end be demonstrated on the basis of other evidence, but this possibility does not provide the evidence itself. Hilberg's critics on this issue have noted that his conclusion logically presupposes comparative analysis—that is, a comparison between the reaction of Jews to the Nazi threat and the reaction of other groups to the same threat—as well as a comparison with the reactions of groups in still other extreme situations. Hilberg does not undertake either of these, and the omission is serious. So, for example, upward of 2 million—according to some accounts, 3.3 million—Russian prisoners of war under Nazi control were killed by execution (in camps or out of them) or by a process of deliberate attrition. Almost all of these were

The Arts of History

men fit enough to serve as soldiers who were held captive on or near their native ground (neither of these advantages were enjoyed by the Jews). Did a *Russian* "strategy" of submission or accommodation account for *their* destruction?

And again, in other extreme situations the common denominator governing reactions of the "victims" has historically been consistently conservative, reverting to strategies employed in the past (echoing the commonplace that generals are always prepared to fight the war just past). This reliance on tradition has been especially evident when the extreme situations noted have no close precedent—in the Black Plague of the fourteenth century, for example, where the "normal" medical procedures contributed to rather than stemmed the death toll, or in the purges following the French Revolution, where large segments of the citizenry, erstwhile revolutionaries themselves, submitted to their own execution rather than react against it. Would these victims have been better off trying different responses, "resisting"? Most probably—but that only reinforces doubts about Hilberg's claim that the Jewish response to the Nazi threat was distinctive (and tainted), a failure of nerve rooted in Jewish history. National or group character is always a difficult and dangerous topic, and for the Holocaust the potential harm of misrepresentation accompanying it increases manifold. Then why chance it? At one point in his memoir/autobiography Hilberg describes himself as having an "allergy" to religion, with Judaism, of course, the example nearest at hand. Allergies are nobody's fault, to be sure, but having revealed this condition, why should he (or his readers) be surprised to find that an allergic reaction has indeed occurred, blurring the otherwise precise historical detail of his work?

It cannot be said, and Hilberg undoubtedly would not want to say, that even balanced against his work as a whole this one issue does not matter. It does matter, and otherwise admiring readers of his may view his statements on this question as not only historically problematic but also morally offensive (for example: "[My use of] the term 'Jewish reactions' refers only to ghetto Jews. This reaction was born in the ghetto and will die there. It is[!] part and parcel of ghetto life. It applies to *all* ghetto Jews, assimilationists and Zionists, the capitalists and socialists, the unorthodox and the religious ones" (*Destruction*, 17). But even granting this distortion full weight does not undo *Destruction*'s distinction or its preeminence in Holocaust historiography. It remains now, almost forty years after its publication, a both historical and contemporary force in thinking about the Holocaust. Everybody concerned with the Holocaust—not only historians—knows this, although others seem readier to accept and build on the fact than Hilberg himself.

And lastly. The deepest and most unusual part of Hilberg's memoir/autobiography concerns not history but the act of writing—again, principally in *Destruction*. Although some historians may still doubt that the process of writing history has anything to do with its substance, the evidence of a reciprocal relation between those two factors has become increasingly difficult to ignore. Any such relation may seem irrelevant to Hilberg because of the mass of numbers and facts, tables and graphs, on which he constructs his narrative; added to the clipped, nonemotive tone of his narrative, these may seem to neutralize anything like the flourishes or individual voice of a style. Impersonal, minimalist, referential—could there be a "harder," more detached prose than Hilberg's? But as literary theorists have found in "realism" a characteristic figurative structure, so Hilberg's severe economy appears under scrutiny to be highly artful: reduced from without by the force of the facts it relates, constrained from within by a recognition that some facts—and some silences—speak for themselves more effectively than whatever might be added to them. Hilberg describes in *The Politics of Memory* his early reading of Genesis in Hebrew with his father, recalling his father's comments on the power of its conciseness. He also speaks of Beethoven's laborious musical constructions (in contrast to the effortlessness of Mozart's creations), likening his own writing to the former, as he too would build "an edifice, draft after draft, slowly, painfully. . . . Beethoven's 'Appasionata' . . . showed me that I could not shout on a thousand pages, that I had to suppress sonority and reverberation, and that I could loosen my grip only selectively, very selectively" (85). A commitment to such principles does not, of course, assure their realization. But recall again the passage cited above from *Destruction* about the "financing" of the deportation to the camps. "For the deportees one-way fare was payable; for the guards a round-trip ticket had to be purchased." What, one asks, could elaboration—commentary or even condemnation—add to a sentence like this? "Above all," Hilberg writes now about his prose, "I was committed to compression."

Hilberg's concern for Holocaust writing does not end with his own. The standards he sets for himself apply also to other authors, for example, to those historians or imaginative writers who subordinate history to extrahistorical goals and who, although professing the severity of their subject, often produce only varieties of kitsch. Perhaps Hilberg would not wish away all Holocaust art, but he mentions none of it approvingly and much of it critically: "The philistines in my field are everywhere. I am surrounded by the commonplace, platitudes, clichés. In sculpture, Jewish resistance fighters are memorialized in the center of Warsaw by a larger heroic statue in Stalinist style [the Rappaport memorial]. In poetry I regularly encounter graves in the sky [undoubtedly a reference to Paul Celan's 'Todesfuge']. In speeches I must listen to man's inhumanity to man." If the work of Celan and Rappaport—and a major theme in theological and philosophical analyses of the Holocaust—are thus excluded, what, we might ask, is left standing? "The manipulation of history is a kind of spoilage, and kitsch is debasement."

What remains must be history *without* "manipulation"—although it is clear that Hilberg does not mean by this untouched by human hands. Certainly it is not history written from the inside by apologists or partisans; nor would it be history written by a neutral or "disinterested" observer. Directly and confrontationally, the historian here would be a moral agent of the history, himself an actor in the drama. Hilberg describes in this memoir/autobiography the fascination that the figure Adam Czerniakow, whose diary he coedited, held for him: "The [Warsaw] ghetto wall marked a sharp separation between perpetrator and victim, but Czerniakow was like a bridge. With him I crossed the boundary, as he went out to hold his official conversations with the Germans and as he returned dejected to the Jewish world. I dwelled with him to grasp his struggle with problems of housing, food, starvation, dues, taxes, and police." Beyond the personal affinity noted in these words, Hilberg evidently views the writing of history as a moral discourse, with the writer as much accountable in his writing about what happened as the more immediate agents of the events described. On the other hand, there is also in this self-narrative—the memoir/autobiography—ample evidence of pettiness and humorlessness, a lack on Hilberg's part of empathy for many of the people to whom he introduces his readers that might evoke for some of his readers William James's notable essay "On a Certain Blindness in Human Beings." Perhaps, one might argue, to write seriously about the perpetrators of the Holocaust will indeed blind the writer in this way; or perhaps the harsh descriptions of the incidents and characters Hilberg encountered on his "journey" are in an unusually strict sense warranted. Even if neither of these applies, moreover, something like the blindness cited by James will surely be familiar to Hilberg's readers. But all this only makes rarer and more important the combination of imagination, patience, and moral passion in the search for hard truths (as both difficult and severe) required to think and to write *The Destruction of the European Jews*. To have realized that combination, it seems, leaves even Hilberg himself still looking back in wonder. But then, what *is* one to do after writing such a book?

107

Goldhagen's Monument to Revenge

Daniel Goldhagen's book *Hitler's Willing Executioners* has caused a remarkable stir, and it has done this under remarkable circumstances. A scholarly and densely (and lengthily) argued book, it has been criticized, often very sharply, by a large majority of "professional" readers (that is, readers who are themselves historians or commentators on the Holocaust). On the other hand, with international sales of more than 500,000 copies, it has obviously struck a popular chord quite unusual for scholarly books whatever their subject, and all the more notable in this case because of the large number of other, more accessible studies of the same subject to which readers can turn. This sharp dichotomy in the book's reception is by now at least as notable as its controversial thesis of the "eliminationist" antisemitism of "ordinary Germans"; the popular reception itself is underscored by the evident difference between the number of people who have bought the book and the number who have actually read it. In order to understand these matters, however, we must look to the book itself—to what it says and, beyond that, to what it represents. I want here to say something about each of these and then about the connection between them.

The central thesis of Goldhagen's book is forthright enough. He contends that the Nazi genocide, the "Final Solution," was a concerted series of acts that involved the collaboration of the German people as a whole and the initiative, within the whole, of a smaller but substantial group of actual "executioners." What produced this extraordinary collaboration—its "necessary and sufficient cause," as Goldhagen is unafraid to designate it—was a particularly virulent and unprecedented strain of antisemitism that was distinctively and even, according to some of his critics, racially, German: "eliminationist antisemitism." All the other talk by historians about the complex causal evolution of the Holocaust—about its economic origins, about the nationalist movements or ethnic tensions that nourished it, about the punitive Versailles treaty or the fatal weakness of the Weimar Republic, even about Hitler's personal obsessions—is in the end for Goldhagen beside the point. Quite simply, the German people were responsible, on cognitive and moral grounds—that is, knowingly and willingly—for the "Final Solution": they shared a demonic and implacable hatred of the Jews, and they acted on it; they did what they did because they wanted and then chose to do it.

What have critics found objectionable in this very forthright thesis? Certainly it has the virtues of simplicity and comprehensibility, but of course it also has the defects of those same virtues. Historians rarely if ever, in the most commonplace circumstances, ascribe necessary and sufficient causes—not as a matter of tradition or even of prudence but because of the improbability of ever fully determining that combination of causes. Indeed, even for much less complex occurrences than the Holocaust—for as rudimentary an act as the choice made in ordering from a restaurant menu—it would require more than just bravado for an observer or even the diner himself to claim knowledge of the "necessary and sufficient" conditions explaining that choice. Furthermore, historians almost never, in tracing the causality behind large-scale events, find themselves arguing for a monocausal ground—again, not so much as a matter of prudence but because of the complexity of the currents of history. Where human agents are involved, even the most elementary acts involve more than a monocausal pattern. When explanations do turn to causes, furthermore, except in the face of extraordinary evidence, they do not exempt reasons themselves from having causes, and often complex ones at that. In other words, the "idea" of antisemitism in any of its varieties would not itself be viewed as autonomous, as formulated apart from a historical and social context, that is, as "immaculately conceived." And this, because *no* ideas come into existence that way.

None of this means that Goldhagen's "eliminationist" thesis could not be true and thus demonstrated, albeit on other or additional grounds. But it does mean that he has an unusually heavy burden of proof to make good on—which, in the eyes of most "professional" readers, he has largely failed to do. Let me give one example, not often remarked even in the many discussions about his book, of how his thesis simplifies (and so distorts) his material for the sake of his polemic. The full title of his volume is *Hitler's Willing Executioners: Ordinary Germans and the Holocaust*. Presumably the first phrase in this sequence has a reference, a denotation. But what is it? Is *executioners* a reference only to actual killers, those who shot or trampled or injected or burned or released the gas pellets? The answer to this must, it seems, be no, since that reference would be at once too narrow and too broad. Too narrow because it would exclude not only figures like Himmler and Eichmann but also the much more numerous and lesser links in the chain of command who also did nothing more violent than give orders; too broad because Goldhagen's reference in the second part of his title to "Ordinary Germans" means that we then have to exclude the many undoubted "executioners" in whom the Nazis found willing allies outside of Germany—in Poland, Lithuania, Latvia, the Ukraine, Croatia (and let us not forget France or Holland).

And then, of course, it is also too broad, since if we agree that the category should not be restricted to actual killers, there is the matter of deciding just how wide the circle should go. When Goldhagen introduces the phrase *ordinary Germans* he suggests an equation between "willing executioners" and "ordinary Germans"; that is, he suggests that the two classes are one and the same, all of the one in the other and all of the other in the one. This would be to say in effect that all "ordinary" (and *a fortiori* extraordinary) Germans bear equal responsibility for the Holocaust. The responsibility assigned in this interpretation is the responsibility of executioners, thus indicting under that charge the 70 million ordinary and extraordinary Germans who populated the Third Reich. More often than not, it seems that Goldhagen means exactly this, forcing an equation, then, among all the many degrees of malevolence and wrongdoing that finally constituted the "Final Solution." But then the question quickly presents itself about the evident differences that such a broad equation must rule out or deny. Perhaps no distinction in terms of "executioners" should be made between the guards (or officials) at the six death "factories" and those at the ten thousand or so "merely" concentration or labor camps. But what of the railroad engineers driving the trains to the camps? the factory workers producing the pellets of the gas Zyklon B or the crematoria in the Topf factory? the owners of these factories? The process of genocide entailed many steps; many feet walked through those steps, and to say that they all were of one kind and one degree suggests the writing of an entirely a priori history, one that would not recognize or admit distinctions even if it found itself in the midst of them.

Goldhagen in his title and at various points in his book suggests this equation, but he carries this on inconsistently, elsewhere admitting or implying the relevance of just such distinctions as they bear on his title. Indeed, he even assigns a number to Hitler's willing executioners, but only once, and then hurriedly and very approximately, as if he would rather not call attention to it. That number, he surmises, would have been between 100,000 and 500,000, although even about this rough estimate of the "willing executioners"—in which he allows himself a more than generous margin of error—there is a good deal to be said. Until late in the war the S.S., which numbered between 800,00 and 900,000 men, was made up entirely of volunteers with a quite explicit ideology. Membership in the Nazi Party itself was also voluntary, and something like 9–10 percent of the German populace joined; at its peak, then, it had on the order of 8 million members. The Party as such was not an organization for executioners, but it obviously served as an important prop for what needed to be done—professionally, socially, industrially, economically—to implement the "Final Solution." And these numbers don't begin to account for the Germans who were so ordinary as not to belong to either of these organizations but still managed to share in the national project. Goldhagen's numbers thus turn out to be arbitrary when they are not simply invisible: they are too small if they are meant to include all the Germans who contributed in some "intimate way" (Goldhagen's phrase) and too large if they refer to the Germans who by some common-sense measure had direct responsibility. But then, it also turns out that such discrepancies hardly matter. For the "willing executioners" were in Goldhagen's view only the ordinary, that is, the typical Germans—exactly like the other Germans who (by chance, it has to be) did not stand in their place at that particular time. What caused them but not the other "ordinary Germans" to become executioners? The same ideal of "eliminationist antisemitism" that they shared with everyone else. So why the one group rather than the other? No particular reason is given for the apparently large difference, an omission suggesting that this apparently large difference also does not matter; perhaps it was only that no additional "willing" and "ordinary" Germans were needed beyond those who did the work. In spirit, however, the collectivity was as one, and thus the German people as a whole—70 million before the outbreak of World War II—qualify for the title "willing executioners," with the lesser numbers that Goldhagen cites on the one occasion mentioned becoming more a gesture to historical propriety than anything else. Much like Hannah Arendt's "banality of evil," which turned Eichmann into a version of Everyman, Goldhagen's "willing executioners" turn out to be all the Germans. And with everyone thus guilty, and equally guilty, not only history but also moral judgment loses any power or right to discrimination.

In posing these objections, I do not mean to deny the difficulty of assigning specific moral responsibility for the Nazi genocide; I agree, furthermore, that collective responsibility is at times a legitimate moral category that may apply to people who are not themselves the immediate or direct agents of an act. But neither of these acknowledgments is strengthened by a refusal to recognize distinctions, first, among the great variety of actions (or inactions) for which "ordinary Germans" were responsible, and then, among their varied motives for those actions or inactions. Goldhagen denies that the first of these distinctions matters, and he denies that the second even exists: All Germans were equally or at least sufficiently responsible. We know this because of the single motive they shared, quite apart from any actions they did or did not contribute to on its basis, that is, the idea (or ideal) of eliminationist antisemitism. Both these denials are, however, distortions; the effect of their exaggeration is to diminish the varieties and indeed the depth of responsibility that ought to be ascribed.

Admittedly the hostile reception of Goldhagen's book on the part of the "experts"—historians, political theorists, culture critics—has involved more than only a reaction against the broad sweep of this central thesis. Some of the intensity of this reaction has probably been due to Goldhagen's severe judgments about his fellow Holocaust historians; in criticizing them, he takes no prisoners and indeed hardly acknowledges that there are prisoners to take. But the weight of scholarly opinion has also been heavily against Goldhagen on substantive grounds. This majority view is not necessarily correct because it is the majority view, of course, but it does highlight the sharp contrast between the popular and laudatory reception of the book and its critical scholarly reception. How are we to understand this radical difference?

One conclusion that might be drawn about this is that the "experts" have relatively little influence outside their own small circle—perhaps in specific relation to Holocaust studies, perhaps more generally, in the diminished role of the intellectual in popular culture. Then again, one might consider also the effective marketing campaign conducted by Knopf, the book's publisher, as well as the narrower explanation—for its harsher critics, a consolation—that like many other "highbrow" trade books, it has surely been much more bought than read. Even if true, however, these accounts do not explain the book's place on the *New York Times* list of bestsellers, its translation into the major European languages (and some lesser ones as well), and its arrival, in Germany of all places, as a major cultural event felt well beyond the circle of historians (with sales of more than 150,000 copies and the award, presented by Jürgen Habermas, of a significant cultural prize). Why? we do well to ask ourselves. I offer as at least a partial explanation a mingling of psychological and moral factors.

In the immediate post-Holocaust years the Nuremberg trials, the still visible devastation of Europe (inside and outside Germany), and the political division of Germany itself conduced to demonstrating to the world that the Germans as a nation had been judged guilty, whether formally or informally, for the war and the atrocities committed in it, among which the genocide of the Jews loomed large. This sweeping judgment was not highly nuanced; the times were hard, and the trauma left by what had transpired was still very much present. The verdict on the past—even at Nuremberg the tribunal singled out individuals— had the unmistakable shape of a collective view of Germany, inclusive in its scope and at least at an abstract level unqualified in its condemnation.

Beginning in the mid-1950s, however—a symbolic landmark here is the signing of the Reparations Agreement between West Germany and Israel—a process of accommodation began. The past was not formally erased, but the framework of historical moral space began to expand to include Germany once again. There was nothing extraordinary about this; short of sentencing the nation of Germany to capital punishment—its destruction—some such development was inevitable. To this complicated mix were added the tensions of the Cold War, in which West Germany was seen by the West as a potentially strong ally, and because of its geography alone, a necessary one. Furthermore, at that time the writing of the history of World War II and of what only then began to be known as the Holocaust also began to take shape. Setting out initially from first-person narratives (diaries, memoirs of horror), more detailed and fully formed histories began to appear in which the lines of analysis that in the first tellings and retellings seemed clear and distinct had now to be quantified and qualified by degrees, to be examined in terms of the technological and bureaucratic complications that the workings of any large-scale mechanism involve. In a nation of 70 million, even with a Führer at its head, policy decisions would have a complex underpinning: Who intended or decided what, when? How much power did they have? What countervailing impulses were there?

Unless one posits a social force as single-minded as Rousseau's "general will," the motives and even the forms of large-scale political decisions will come in shades of grey, not in black and white; this means that moral judgments on them, readily made when what they are deciding between are also as distinct as black and white, must be similarly muted. Is recognition of the complexity and, often, unclarity of historical causality a defect in writing history? Not in itself—if only because there is no credible alternative. But it does weaken the force of moral categories for which it is precisely the large distinctions that matter most, beginning with the rudimentary ones between right and wrong, good and evil. Goldhagen writes in a tradition that joins the historical polemic to an edifying moralism, and if there is a range of authors, from Edmund Burke to Karl Marx, who manage that combination more skillfully than he does, this is nothing against the tradition itself. Goldhagen demonstrates, however, that even the "normal" hyperbole of the polemic or the tendentiousness of the edifying discourse can be exaggerated or caricatured, with the effect of undermining the very position he advocates. That moral judgment can—must—also be cognitive, of the head as well as of the heart, is no doubt a hard lesson to learn—but a still harder one to ignore.

A half-century after the Holocaust, many observers of that event—its contemporaries and the generations after them—have come to feel that the responsibility—the guilt—of Germany has somehow been forgotten, diffused, obscured. Certainly by those who want to forget it but even by those who want, for themselves and others, to remember. This last irony cannot be avoided: the same historical scholarship on which so much of the "memory" and future of the Holocaust depends—at some near point in the future, on which the dependence of memory will be total—may, despite and against itself, have the effect not quite of erasure but of the near-equivalent of inundation: burying even that distinctive event under the detail of historical studies, which have always to be set in context, qualified, nuanced, precise. And so there is no avoiding, nor reason to want to avoid, accounts of voting patterns among the different economic classes in Germany's pre-Hitler elections, or of the process of decision making in the hierarchies of the German Lutheran or Catholic churches (and in the hierarchies of the professional medical or juridical associations), or of the more decisive but no less intricate and often ambiguous processes of military strategies and tactical planning.

Numerous Holocaust memorials have been built to honor its victims, but where—the question forces itself—are the memorials that condemn, and remind their viewers to condemn, the perpetrators? Monuments that serve the first purpose do not—cannot—serve the second. So where do we find those others? Why are they absent? What would they be? It is here that I believe we find the purpose and role of Goldhagen's book, the void it was intended to fill, the impulse in him of which the book was an expression and which, as expression of the same impulse, has brought him his warm reception outside the scholarly community, among the world of "common" readers. This response, again, has been epitomized in Germany itself, where the book has allowed a younger generation, and by now more than one—the postwar generations—to settle scores with the older one: a common intergenerational pattern that is here intensified by the eagerness of that particular older generation *not* to speak or hear of the past and their role in it. Goldhagen's writing is thus best understand, it seems to me, as a monument—one which just happens to be shaped like a book. It is proposed, no doubt, as a monument to justice, but it stands more exactly as a monument to revenge. "Remember Amalek," the biblical text resonates, and Goldhagen has found a way to commemorate the new Amalek in a new kind of memorial. Few will view his monument without some sense of recognition or identification. But that sense is in the heart, not the head—a distinction Goldhagen is unwilling to make but one that cannot be denied even in shaping a monument.

Second Sight: Shimon Attie's Recollection

Shimon Attie's representations of the Holocaust are as distinctive ontologically as they are aesthetically. He projects onto the buildings of what in the 1930s was a predominantly Jewish section of Berlin, the Scheunen Quarter (under the Yiddish rubric "Finstere Medine" [dark country]), the images of those buildings with all the signs of life that then inhabited them. The bearded faces, the Hebrew lettering on shop windows—all these are superimposed as images on the now almost entirely *Judenfrei* buildings, some of them postwar constructions, some the very ones photographed in the 1930s but with a great difference. So the projected images of the past rest on the actuality of the present. Attie leaves the projected images there for a Berlin audience to see for a short time, but having photographed them, he also leaves them for the permanent record, which we, far from Berlin, are able to examine. Thus, the question of where Attie's art works *are* is more difficult to answer than it would be if applied to more conventional art, like paintings or poems. But at least we have the photographic record of his installations, and the photographs themselves, however we classify them among the genres of art, speak in their own and distinctive voice.[2]

To be sure, as photographs of photographs of photographs, they offer the difficult combination of a Platonic nightmare and an artist's dreamworld. There is the temptation, then, to turn to Attie's own statements about his work for clues to how to "read" them, that is, how to understand his visual (and vivid) images in the terms he himself sets. But this, of course, is just what the "Intentional Fallacy" is meant to warn us *against,* as it urges us to do what most viewers—at least until they become critics—would spontaneously do anyway, that is, to look at art's images in the present, *their* present, quite apart from what the artist, whose gifts may not be with words at all, tells us that he sees or what we should be seeing.

We have, then, to make our own way here, although, admittedly, only insofar as we assume the fact of the Holocaust as the causal clue required even to begin to understand Attie's visual projections and installations. In these works, Attie engages a number of important general issues set in motion by the very conception of "Holocaust images" or "Holocaust art," with its provocative consequences for the interrelations between form and content, the aesthetic and the ethical, the particular (or historical) and the universal (that is, the aesthetic *or* the ethical). I can here only point to certain implications of these relations for —and from—the concept of Holocaust art, indicating why they are

2. Shimon Attie, *The Writing on the Wall: Projections in Berlin's Jewish Quarter* (Heidelberg: Edition Braus, 1994).

important for aesthetic theory and how they take shape in Attie's remarkably imaginative work.

I hasten to add that in this context the phrase "remarkably imaginative," is meant only in part as laudatory; indeed, I shall be proposing here, as I have elsewhere, that certain subjects or occasions of art benefit from less rather than from more imagination, or to put the matter still more bluntly, that art may itself at times be a menace to art. And more specifically, with reference to Attie himself, that certain vectors coming out of his work verge on this danger, the more precariously because we encounter them not very far from the apex of his work's power. The same tendencies, I believe, disclose the anatomy of the moral and historical burden of art more generally—specifically, then, of Holocaust art but in the end of art as such.

In an earlier essay in this volume (Chapter 2) I paraphrased a line by Walter Pater to read that "All Holocaust literature aspires to the condition of history." This gloss was meant to suggest that imaginative writing about the Holocaust often, even typically, eschews standard literary devices or figures in favor of historical ones—purporting to present factual narratives that are not factual at all, inserting chunks of juridical testimony into fictional frames, appealing to historical genres like the diary or letter or memoir, but as imagined not historical means, in poetry violating literary convention not only in order to be unconventional but to be unpoetic, and in the medium of film disguising its virtuoso powers under the more severe constraints of the documentary (a small example of this last point is Spielberg's conceit in *Schindler's List* of using black-and-white film rather than color).

There is, it seems to me, nothing mysterious or even subtle about this historicizing impulse. For the representation of moral enormity on the scale of genocide, artistic sensibility and imagination might well defer to the weight of history and *its* "story." It seems obvious that artists would—should—hardly think of the ideal of beauty in addressing the subject of the Holocaust. Even so far as concerns the representation of evil or cruelty, history as it emerges transformed after the "Final Solution" has proved to be every bit as inventive as the artistic imagination ever was; the historical record shows that its own creators, the Nazis themselves, required time and strenuous effort before they realized exactly what it was they were creating in the "artifact" of genocide. And it follows from such considerations that, given the moral pressure exerted by this subject, perhaps not uniquely but extraordinarily, the usual risks run by art in imaginatively heightening or revising perception, in taking the aesthetic turn, increase substantially.

All these factors might be good reasons for regarding photography, Attie's basic instrument, as a privileged medium in taking the Holocaust as a subject for art. For to whatever extent one emphasizes the creative or aesthetic process of photography, its distinctive and certainly disproportionate referentiality in comparison with other visual or, for that matter, literary arts is evident. Admittedly, the schools or movements that have been categorized under the generic title "realism" have surfaced in virtually all the arts, in literature and even in music as well as in painting. But when Roland Barthes in *Camera Lucida* characterizes the photograph as not a "copy" but an "emanation" (see Chapter 1), he invokes, I think convincingly, something more basic than the terms of only one more artistic trope or genre. "It is often said," he writes, "that it was the painters who invented photography. . . . I say: no, it was the chemists. . . . The photograph is literally an emanation of the referent. From a real body, which was there, proceed radiations which ultimately touch me, who am here."[3] And indeed certain photographs (and documentary clips) from the Holocaust have become standard, I'm tempted to say rigid, designators of the Holocaust in a way paralleled by very few of its other representations (some of the most evocative of which—the diaries of Anne Frank and Emmanuel Ringelblum, for example—are also "emanations," albeit literary ones).

All this, however, applies to photography initiated in the Holocaust past, with figures or events embodied there themselves now past, gone, over. And so one might imagine—it *requires* imagining, since the conventions by themselves halt at this point—the question of whether anything can be done to reassert in the present, our present, the nonfigurative realism, the immediacy, of a presence that Barthes ascribes to photography in its relation to the past. Only such a means, it seems, could

<hr>

3. Roland Barthes, *Camera Lucida*, trans. Richard Howard (New York: Hill & Wang, 1981), 80.

effect a passage between the Scylla of artistic fancy(does anyone now require a "moving experience" of the Holocaust?) and the Charybdis of didactic abstraction(exactly what is gained by hearing once again about the "unimaginable" nature of the Holocaust?), both these temptations threatening to turn the images of that subject into clichés.

It is precisely at this point that Shimon Attie's work seems to accomplish what much other Holocaust art does not: to bring the terms of that event in the past into the present without diminishing or rationalizing either at the expense of the other. An instructive connection appears here, in both likeness and difference, between Attie's work and Claude Lanzmann's film *Shoah*. Lanzmann also sought to connect the past and the present by the artistic means of absence; he viewed the Shoah not by revisiting or reconstructing its records, that is, not by presenting images from the past, but by conveying the imprint of that past through voices speaking in the present, the voices of survivors, perpetrators, bystanders—through all of whom the past was then to be inferred. What this amounted to was an artistic enthymeme to which the viewer was then to supply the conclusion: the "veterans" of the Holocaust summoning now, by way of the marks it had left on them, the events they endured or (for the perpetrators) caused. In Attie's work, especially in his "Finstere Medine," to which I principally refer, the viewer is confronted not only with images taken from the past but also with their iteration in the present, staking a claim to the same spaces that they had once had but that are now quite differently occupied. That is, to show the past *in* the present.

Admittedly, the images that Attie projects of the past—the shops and shopkeepers, the residents, passersby—constitute only a virtual present. But their imposition on actual space marks a more than virtual addition of the past to the actual present: the *addition* now, rather than the subtraction that images of the past more typically impose. The main focus of images and interpretations of the Holocaust—in art and historiography, in its memorials as well as in its analysis—has been on palpable loss. Auschwitz has become a metonymy not only for all six of the "death camps," but for the 10,000 concentration camps, for the "Final Solution" as a whole, and then for the act of genocide as such. It is important, however, to recognize another view of the loss inflicted

The Arts of History

by these events, a loss that was by its nature less palpable but in the end is not less actual or a source of harm; this is the view of what would have existed—lived, grown, worked, thrived—if the Holocaust had not occurred. Of course, there is no way of knowing the details of this existence, even the numbers, let alone the identities of those to whom it would have given life. But Attie's "Finstere Medine" gives body and definition, a human reality, to the shapes and spaces that those who disappeared would have occupied—replacing them if only by a virtual, but then not only virtual, image. This is the dialectical conclusion that emerges from his imposition of the photographic image of Jewish life in Berlin-past on life without Jews in Berlin-present.

I have been emphasizing the "Finstere Medine" rather than Attie's other projects mainly because that work's historical insistence and forcefulness—the limits it imposes on the imagination and thus the means of its sharp focus—seem to me more striking than the later examples of his *oeuvre* cast in the same mold. To be sure, the later photographs also take on agency, not only making themselves available to the viewer but also causing the viewer to engage them. But the faces projected at the Dresden railroad station, photographs of the Jewish deportees from that station, require more than they or their viewers can provide, and the subtext that has to be supplied seems bound to diminish the point of the projection if not to divert the viewers from it entirely. (This tactic—the assumption of a historical subtext in their ahistorical images—is a common feature of many strong Holocaust artists who, like Attie, require their audiences to supply the correlative of the "Final Solution." Consider how impoverished an understanding would result without that subtext in the poetry of Paul Celan, the novels of Aharon Appelfeld, even in the more nearly explicit paintings of Anselm Kiefer. It was Appelfeld who explained this tactic of indirection by an analogy: "One does not," he wrote, "look directly at the sun.")

Earlier in this discussion I suggested that my reference to the "remarkably imaginative" quality of Shimon Attie's work was not entirely laudatory. What I meant by that qualification concerns the balance within the binary pairs whose conjunction Attie, like most Holocaust artists, constantly invokes: ethical judgment in relation to aesthetic appreciation, the status of the particular (or historical) event in relation to its universal or abstract implication. And the danger intrinsic to those polarities seems to me one that impairs even Attie's notable achievement insofar as he often pushes farther toward the second pole than his subject warrants and perhaps can bear.

For example, Attie himself reports that not all the slides from the Holocaust past that he projected onto buildings in the present were superimposed on their original sites; more than that, not all the slides of past scenes were photographs from the Scheunen Quarter or even from Berlin. In other words, he has conceded that if his viewers regard his photographic superimpositions as historically veracious, they will sometimes be mistaken; certain of the buildings, shops, and pedestrians now seen could not have been seen where he projects them. But, we might well ask, what difference does this make? After all, it is truly *that* past which is projected onto the present, if not in direct reflection on the present. Attie himself anticipates this question. Far from detracting from his project, he suggests, this historical conflation increases its effectiveness: where he had to choose between being a good historian and a good artist, he writes in his comments on the "Finstere Medine," he "always chose the latter."

But is the justification for that choice, or even for the distinction between history and art on the grounds he assumes, so obvious? Surely there might be loss, not gain, in the consciousness of artifice. Suppose, for example, that Primo Levi's account of his year in Auschwitz, *Survival in Auschwitz*, or of his lengthy journey back to Italy once the war was over, *The Reawakening*, turned out to be a composite of his own and other peoples' experience, with some of the events "only" imagined; or that the accounts retold by the figures in Lanzmann's *Shoah* were in fact amalgams of various partial histories stitched together. Most recently, why is anyone troubled by the discovery that Benjamin Wilkomirski could not have experienced the events he relates in his much-praised "memoir," *Fragments?* It might be argued that the addition of art to history in these cases has had a stronger impact on audiences than either one of that pair would have had by itself, especially if history had been made to stand on its own. Well, perhaps—but certainly not if the audience had first been given to understand that the

The Arts of History

works involved were not such syntheses, and arguably not even if the audience had been aware beforehand of the possibility. It might be objected that in the absence of information provided from external sources, there would be no way internally of distinguishing fact from fiction in Attie's work or in work similar to it. And if this was the case, the question would then go on, why should any external evidence that might be brought to bear make any difference when it is the text, after all, that is the thing? Well, again, perhaps—but also unlikely. Does not just knowing even the possibility of the two alternatives, like the possibility of forgery in paintings, make a difference in the way one observes them, especially for those works whose provenance seems to be beyond question? (It is, after all, the truly successful forgeries that have passed unquestioned.) The "reliable narrator" so important in certain fictional literary genres is arguably no less so in the memoir or autobiography; here too, after all, the work's power draws fundamentally on the chemical aura of photography.

This issue of imagining arises in slightly different form in certain other statements by Attie as well. He has written that he does not consider himself a "Holocaust artist," and I understand him in saying this to refer mainly to the absence from his work of scenes depicting the manifold horrors of that event. In the account I have been giving, however, this absence, far from removing him from the association of Holocaust artists, places him in good standing among them. For Attie is far from alone in resisting a critical categorization based on the subject of his work. To be sure, he might also mean something else by this objection, and we have some indication of this when he elsewhere describes the subject of his work not as the Holocaust, not "about" the Nazis or the Jews in particular, but as man's inhumanity to man, the ways in which people commit acts of barbarism and cruelty against others. He moves in this direction more explicitly in his later work, for example, in the Denmark project—the series of underwater lights placed in Copenhagen's harbor. The sea rescue of the Danish Jews who were transported by their countrymen to Sweden in 1943, which is the "manifest" occasion of this work, turns out in his view to evoke also the plight of "present day boat-refugees." And so too in the Krakow project, where he links the photographs of the prewar city to "post-Com-

munist Poland's struggle . . . with both old and new forms of racism."
Attie proposes these "readings" of his work, although in both instances
the photographs of Jews in the pre-Holocaust period stand at the center, impelling the project forward. Why, one asks, the constancy of that
one source if indeed it is suffering *humanity* that is its focus?

Always of course, and irrespective of their particular subject, artists
must decide how and where to circumscribe that subject, which of its
elements they choose to display and which of its implications to emphasize. Furthermore, the cognate question for the viewer—how to de- 123
termine what a particular text is "about"—recurs, since any work can
be given alternative descriptions, set at different levels of generality as
well as viewed from quite different perspective. (Consider, for example, the Holocaust as viewed by a historian of Madagascar, that near
fictional area of relocation for the Jews, as it was briefly considered by
the Nazi hierarchy prior to the "Final Solution.") But to answer the
question, What is the subject of *King Lear?* by saying that the subject
is a king named Lear would itself be blind—as the alternative reach for
that handy tool of literary appreciation, the "human condition," would
remain quite empty.

There should, it seems, be a way of mediating between the raw particular and the abstract universal that comes closer to the work in its
significance—and as its specific subject exerts more pressure sometimes at one end of that spectrum, sometimes at the other. This is one
way, it seems, that content may—must—act on form. And in the case
of the Holocaust, that content, with its flagrant particularity—specifically, the Nazis and their allies attempting to destroy, also specifically,
the Jews—is endangered, artistically as well as morally. Artistically *because* morally—by the push toward universalization. This is, I suggest,
an important element of Adorno's warning about the barbarism of
writing (and, one supposes, reading) poetry after Auschwitz that warrants continued attention; it points to the danger faced by any work,
including Attie's, that uses aspects of the Holocaust as an idiom or even
metaphor for the many other dark events and sides of human history
or character.

To introduce the content-form relation in this context suggests the
possible claim that for some subjects or contents no artistic form may

be adequate; that is, that art could not (and because of that, should not try to) represent them. Any such claim will undoubtedly be a red flag to the widespread inclination now to give art a virtual, that is, an actual, carte blanche—the benefit of clergy that the clergy themselves do not now often enjoy. Art in these postromantic terms has, or admits, no limits on either its content or its form. But once we accept the persistent thesis of aesthetics that art involves a strong, arguably intrinsic relation between form and content, then the possibility is entailed that the balance between form and content is variable not only in respect to those elements within a single work but as such, that is, within the domain of art as a whole. The denial of this extension to the process of representation or to images as such would invite artistic and, depending on its ground, moral failing. The possibility that content may exceed any possible form has been cogently argued in accounts of the Sublime (e.g., by Kant) that emphasize its links to the moral domain, with the Sublime in these terms evidence as well as expression of man's moral capacity and grandeur. Why, then, should this same possibility be ruled out for its inverse, the *evil* Sublime? These last comments are not directed against Shimon Attie's work as a whole or against the "Finstere Medine," which in itself bears comparison with the most acclaimed visual work by Holocaust artists. But they do clash with other of his work, as well as with what he says about it. He too might agree, however, that in the end an audience should trust the tale, not the teller—a principle that places a substantial burden on each of them, especially where the tale told is the Holocaust.

Translating the Holocaust   7

For Whom Does One Write?

Act and Idea in the Nazi Genocide was first published in 1990. I began to write the book a decade before that with two purposes in mind. The first of these came from my belated awareness of the violent absence caused by the Nazi genocide against the Jews—in the worldwide historical and moral space emptied by the "Final Solution" but also, more locally for me, in the small Connecticut town where I grew up during the years when that event unfolded. There, close to the ocean, where summer beachgoers clustered, while on its other shore genocide was being imagined and committed—the idea and the act—a first- and second generation Jewish community looked backward to prewar Europe for its social and religious inheritance, forward to the American "melting pot" for the business and professional lives of its children, with little more than a sideward glance at the destruction enveloping the Jews of Europe and the *shtetlach* that had been their own not long before.

I could hardly infer from this personal history a general charge of indifference in the American Jewish community during the years of the

Written as an introduction to the Hebrew translation of *Act and Idea in the Nazi Genocide* (Jerusalem: Magnes, 2000).

Nazi genocide. But about my own history and its protective coating I have no doubts. Certainly at the time—in the early 1940s—for a young boy to find himself Jewish in small-town America evoked mainly a combination of the warmth of an extended family through the closely knit Jewish community and the excitement of new-found freedoms that were recognizable even to those of us who had never experienced the restraints or threats of the Old World that our parents or, for me, grandparents had thought to escape. These reactions were intensified rather than dampened by the mark of difference that being Jewish carried with it even in that sleepy New England setting, a mark apparently evident to everyone although outwardly invisible and, except for the occasional name-calling and schoolyard fights that initiated me into this worldly tradition, without consequence.

126

We never know fully, of course, what it is that colors the images we have of the past. But since all we know of the past comes by observing it from the perspective of the present, we are bound to follow the lines that link the two, and my own view of the connections between those terminals has hardly altered despite the growing distance between them. Not many tensions or disturbances affected the small Jewish community as I knew it; the few that did occur were focused on the community itself, minor enough even in their own terms to prove that they were indeed local: the turnover among teachers at the local Hebrew school, fundraising for the synagogue (and for the blue-and-white boxes of the Jewish National Fund), disagreements about the degree of kashruth maintained by the three local butchers. It was, in any event, only thirty years later, in the late 1970s and early 1980s—breaking into the usually calm surface of my work as a teacher of philosophy, with my thinking and writing there further abstracted by the designs of aesthetics and the philosophy of art—that I began to realize how insulated and detached those early years had been, not only because a young boy *would* be less intent on world history than on growing into himself but also because even during the war years the Jewish community in town found its own self-absorption possible and, more significantly, natural. Up to the point where they impinged on each other, the town and the Jewish community were full worlds in themselves; when they touched, they saw in each other's reflection a powerful combination of sameness and difference that left little incentive for traveling farther. Why, after all, should someone able to look from that boundary in both directions at once imagine or desire anything more?

But my awareness of this quality in the past—and of its danger— did not surface as only a personal "recovered" memory. By the 1970s, historical evidence had accumulated of the muted response within the American Jewish community as a whole during the years of the Nazi genocide, findings that reinforced my own slimmer recollection of the same silence and, as it seems, failure. This broader evidence underscored the sense I had of an obligation to close that gap, most immediately for myself but in effect for anyone who had been the beneficiary of the illusory peace that kept that war within a war at a distance. (Nobody in America could ignore the larger war—Pearl Harbor, the draft, rationing, the gold stars in windows.)

To be sure, no reaching back into history enables us to undo or redo it. But it is possible to project the present into the past and, to this extent, bring the two face-to-face. And so I envisioned the book I then began to write as an effort, futile as it must be because of the hard facts it would face, to turn whatever skills and knowledge I had acquired toward filling a space that I knew could never be made whole. That effort itself, moreover, did not come without doubts. Retrospective charges of moral failure turn easily into cant, and certainly such claims appear more readily after the events they challenge than at the time of the events themselves: the past viewed from the present is manageable in a way that the present itself is not. And then, too, there is the accompanying temptation to reflect on such events by looking backward as a substitute for acting on their consequences in the present.

But if reflection is sometimes only a means of avoidance or displacement, it may also disclose facts that have to be reckoned with. Thus, other "post-Holocaust" evidence has shown that it was not only my small hometown or even the larger American Jewish community that earned the lasting scrutiny of judgment; Jewish communities elsewhere also stood under the same shadow: North and South America, the countries of Europe in which the Jewish populace retained a measure of autonomy, the Yishuv in what was then Palestine. Regarding them all, it is impossible to avoid the conclusion that their members could have done more than they did for their (often literally) brethren facing the Nazi menace. Not in the vacuous sense that something more can always be done than most of us do in answer to our obligations, but more directly, in recognizing specific steps—efforts at levels high and low—that might have been taken against the unfolding act of the Nazi genocide, initiatives that could have been attempted but were not.

Not everybody is made to be a soldier; fewer people still have in them the stuff of heroes. But there is nobody who cannot from a distance place himself in opposition, speak out. And often not even this was attempted. One would like to think that should a comparable threat arise now, the reaction among the world's Jewish communities would be different. But we know too that the lessons people learn from history have themselves an uneven history; this is itself a lesson that adds weight to the better-known dangers of judging or moralizing backwards. Yet, however numerous the pitfalls in making the past accountable to the present, there are greater dangers still in refusing to take the risk—that is, if the past is to be recalled with accuracy.

Admittedly, the charge of detachment or indifference to the Nazi genocide applies no less widely to the "peoples of the world"—including the Allied powers, who, although directly engaged in fighting the Nazis, nonetheless refused, with only minor exceptions, to alter their immigration policies in a way that might provide havens for those facing the Nazi death threat. It holds also for the "neutral" states of Europe, who, as we are now still learning, used that special status as a justification for looking away, that is, for not seeing what they saw. But weighty as the evidence is of this broader neglect, it should not be a pretext now for Jewish communities to forget the responsibility that was theirs. Nor should these extended charges be interpreted as so diffusing responsibility as to leave everybody—and as it would then be, nobody—culpable. For again, there were specific actions that the "bystander" nations of the world, much like individual persons, could have initiated that they did not; it is no less clear—and more to the point—that there were specific actions that Jewish communities themselves could have initiated but did not, actions that might have diminished the unfolding harm.

The claim has been argued in serious historical critiques that no matter what efforts had been made by the Allies or the "bystander" countries or the Jewish communities outside occupied Europe, such efforts would not have altered the outcome—that by the time sufficient evidence of the "Final Solution" was known, during the later months of 1942, much of the apparatus of destruction directed against the Jews, and much of the destruction itself, was irreversible and thus that whatever could have been accomplished would at best have made only a marginal difference. On this account, the limited ability of the Allied powers to deflect Nazi policies and actions; still more, the constraints on the "neutral" countries; and even more than that, the political weakness of the Jewish communities outside of Europe, including the Yishuv in Palestine—would have meant that little would be accomplished even if those groups had initiated the concerted attempts at resistance or rescue or protest that they did not. But no one can be certain of this counterfactual prediction—against which there is also, even in its own terms, substantial counterevidence. And still more important, the moral principle has continually to be faced that responsibility depends not only on outcomes or consequences but also—arguably, more basically—on intention and will. It is there that a large part of the historical failure lay and remains still, and in a sense always, to be reckoned with.

It thus seemed to me in writing *Act and Idea*, as it does now too, with its publication for a Hebrew-speaking audience, that if this part of the past is to matter for the present, the focus of thinking or writing the Shoah must be on these basic elements of moral responsibility—on what could and should have been attempted by those individuals and groups who even in those constrained circumstances retained a certain freedom of response but evidently refused to act on it. Such reflection need not emphasize the placing of "blame," although there is also no way, or reason, to avoid that. More important for this analysis, however, is the understanding it may provide of how the destruction succeeded in extending as far as it did—thus, in identifying the contributory factors around the central and decisive intention of Nazi policy itself. So, as I thought about this goal, I would turn my own efforts toward it, hoping to strengthen a link between the present and the past, and then also between them and the future.

But what could philosophical inquiry add to our knowledge or understanding of the act of genocide beyond the ground laid by the historians, who, after all, begin from and return to its hard facts—facts that indeed speak for themselves if any facts ever have? This question produced the second of my intentions in writing *Act and Idea*. For philosophers themselves have repeatedly disagreed over whether what they do, their methods or conclusions, have anything like a distinctive character, whether philosophy constitutes or yields a body of knowledge undetected by other disciplines or methods. Claims that affirm or deny this view have changed little from their earliest appearance in the quarrels between Plato and the Sophists, but at least one general conclusion has emerged from this contentious history: even on the assumption of a distinctive philosophical form or content of discourse—still more, if the opposite is assumed—there is no way to predict where, for any particular problem, such analysis will lead. I undertook the writing of *Act and Idea*, then, with the hope—but also in uncertainty—that philosophy as I spoke for or about it could advance the understanding of an event that, although known corporately, most commonly as "The Holocaust," included so many disparate and often discordant parts that any hope for a single representation encompassing them all must be given up by anyone who seriously considered the matter. The large and continually growing number of writings about the Nazi genocide, a number that continues its rate of increase outside even more than inside Israel, attests, it seems to me, not only to their common moral purpose, which each person would be obliged to attempt to realize for himself, but to the unlikelihood that any one such account could possibly "get it right."

Beyond this uncertainty, I was also aware that philosophy faced another difficulty in the relation of its manner or method to its "implied readers." For philosophical writing typically assumes its own universal applicability—that what it asserts will hold true, if it is true at all, for all times and places, irrespective of cultural or historical differences. And insofar as philosophy holds this ideal, it also assumes a correspondingly ideal and universal understanding on the part of its audience. In other words, it would ascribe to its readers a network of "incidental" identities—their political or religious or social affiliations, where they live, what languages they speak—that make no essential difference to their comprehension or power of judgment. In these terms, the faculty of understanding, even moral understanding, is a human capacity, whatever cultural or historical differences provide a language for that capacity.

This image of an ideal or universal reader, however, depends on assumptions that are not at all self-evident—an objection relevant also to the publication of *Act and Idea* in Hebrew as now a national as well as an international language. For it is impossible to ignore the fact that readers in Israel, where the book now appears, will bring to their reading, beyond personal differences, the histories and allegiances of varied, sometimes conflicting backgrounds (including that of a substantial Hebrew-speaking Arab populace). About some of these groups I have little more than "newspaper" knowledge, and I have not tried to anticipate where the differences between them (or within them) might lead even for the central subject addressed here, the "act and idea" constituting the Nazi genocide. This limitation does not mean that understanding is a function only of the individual culture; the fact of the Nazi genocide itself seems to me to refute this. But it is also clear that in order to grasp that, or any, complex historical event involving personal or group identity among its agents or objects, we have to recognize the different reactions to it in which variant perspectives on the event may conclude. If history is to be more than only ideology or fiction, it must also be transcultural and interpersonal, and this means that far from ignoring or overriding differences in perspective, we have to take them into account, indeed to account *for* them.

On the other hand, if there is a certain irony in the weight added by the Hebrew translation of my book to the question of whom the book was originally addressed to or written for, that same question would be inescapable without the addition of a new audience. Did I originally intend to write about the Nazi genocide for a specifically American Jewish audience? For the "world" Jewish audience? For, or more precisely, against, that collective of "liberal" readers who have been tempted to dissolve the politics of the Nazi genocide by hoping to revive the principles of Enlightenment thinking? But to address the book deliberately to any or even, concentrically, to all of these "parti-

Translating the Holocaust

san" groups would render its conclusions tendentious. How then could the book simply be translated from one language to another as if neither the languages nor other differences among the speakers (that is, the readers) of those languages made any difference to the "meaning" of the text?

This impediment to the possibility of translation is all the more pointed for *Act and Idea* because of a specific thesis I defend in it. For in contrast to many accounts of the Nazi genocide that in the end conceive that event in "universal" terms—as proof of what "man is capable of doing to man"—I argue that any such general claim obscures the essential feature of the genocide, namely, its specificity, that is, its assault by one group of people on another, also particular, group. To transpose this quite specific relation onto an abstract and equivocal "human" background may have a certain force, but it also invites what seems to me the greater danger of losing sight of its own origins. For the Nazi genocide was initiated by one exclusionary group, the Nazis, against another specific group, the Jews; even more than this, it was initiated because of a conception of specificity, that is, because of the identity ascribed by the Nazis to Jews as Jews and because of the singularity in the Nazis' conception of that identity and their will to deny its legitimacy or, more simply, its actuality.

To be sure, the two groups that came to be connected in this way shared a common humanity, notwithstanding the denial of that relation by one of them. But it was not this common humanity that forced the issue between the two or that caused what happened to happen; quite the contrary. Thus, to view the attack by the one on the other at the level of "human" abstraction is to misrepresent the event itself, not only historically, where the distortion is obvious, but also conceptually and morally, where the distortion, if not obvious, is demonstrable. Admittedly, general or universal claims may apply to individuals and to one-time events. But there is a difference between introducing such claims for the sake of drawing universal conclusions and using them to arrive at a particular directive for action, as in the denial of universality or commonality that shaped the Nazi genocide. This denial—the refusal to allow a place for Jewish particularity, that is, to deny Jewish existence—was decisive in the genocide's "act and idea." Had it not been asserted, there would have been nothing for this book to be written about. But since it was asserted, and since the book was then to be written, the specificity at the heart of the issue should be recognizable in the writing about the subject as well as in the subject itself.

And what then of the related feature of the author's own voice? I have already mentioned the "place"—both literal and metaphorical—from which I wrote. As much as this goes against the conventional wisdom that supposes both a common ground for all experience and the universal reach of philosophical discourse, it seems clear that there is a difference—that there could hardly not be—between the act of writing about the Nazi genocide by someone who writes as a Jew and the act of writing about that subject by someone who is not a Jew—perhaps not an indefeasible difference but nonetheless a significant one. And so there would also be a related difference in the reading of such writings. A comparable, albeit deeper contrast distinguishes what the survivor of an experience brings to his representation of it and the reflections of someone who, whatever his powers of empathy, only observed what those he writes about underwent. Of course, experience alone does not ensure the power of expression, but neither does the power of expression ensure authenticity. The partiality of any personal or group identity shapes the future no less than the past, and since even writing about the past is always "for" the future, partiality will be unavoidable also for those writers who are most strongly committed to the ideal of disinterest, an ideal that is itself, after all, part of the history of "interests." Thus both the past and the future experience of writers and readers shape their present roles. Either of those sides of the temporal line may be turned or affected by a text, although other factors are also invariably at work. It is unlikely that a reader who reads a book for a second time after a ten-year interval will find it the "same" book he read earlier, and if this is true for a single person, it seems reasonable to expect still larger differences over time within a variegated culture.

Undoubtedly, lesser differences than many others that separate them distinguish the response of American Jews who address the Nazi genocide from the response of Israeli Jews who address the same subject. But that distinction is nonetheless substantial. Minimally, it affects the particular questions a writer chooses to raise and then the responses and emphases given them. I have already mentioned, for example, the special relevance for Israeli history of the Yishuv's response in Mandate Palestine to news of the Jewish destruction in Eastern Europe (from which, at the time, the majority of Yishuv members had come). In the last decade a number of books have appeared in Israel that confront this question with a directness and severity that was absent previously. An important feature of those accounts is their description of a conflict within the Yishuv between the interests of building a new state and the efforts subordinated to that goal that might have been aimed at the defense and rescue of European Jews, a conflict that was long muted in public discussion and that, whatever judgment one makes on it, remains a serious issue.

A second "inner-directed" question concerns the causal relation between the newly independent State of Israel in 1948 and the Nazi genocide that ended in 1945. This relationship too has been the subject of considered discussion in Israel in recent years, with positions at the two extremes claiming that the Nazi genocide had either nothing or everything to do with the establishment of the state—the *T'kumah*. There have been a number of intermediate views between these extremes— although on this point the admission of any causal connection has significant implications for the more general conclusion. I did not ignore this issue in the book: the status of Zionism and the "ingathering" of the Exile is at least as urgent a question for Jews outside of Israel as for those within it. But I did not address it in the detail that the question warrants. Still more pertinently (and contentiously), the position I take on the theoretical issues at stake in this question at once affirms both the significance of Israel in contemporary Jewish existence, rooted for me personally in the several years I lived there, and the viability of Jewish communal existence outside Israel, of which I have also been a part. What appears in such terms to be contradictory is, as I conceive it, quite consistent. But even aside from this particular view, the more general phenomenon of having English turned into Hebrew discloses the possibility that differences in the social identity of writers (or readers) will also make a difference in their assessments of what is written about (and then translated). Thus, determining the causal relation between the Nazi genocide and the creation or independence of Israel is not the apparently straightforward matter of establishing "the facts" within that circumscribed space and time. It involves a conception of the prior history of the Yishuv and its relation to both the Jewish Diaspora and the non-Jewish nations and communities, which in turn involves differences not only in respect to past interests but also in respect to commitments for the future that may still more markedly divide individuals or groups. What is historically possible at any particular moment, even if partly indeterminate, is itself part of the historical record. And unless one seriously considers what might have been in place of what *is* now, an issue that requires more than only historical deliberation, the question of what was possible in the past becomes easily obscured.

And then, still more generally, there is the question that includes but extends beyond the first two, that of the incorporation of the Nazi genocide in Israeli collective memory—the question of how, in the fifty-year "post-Holocaust" period, the destruction of the European Jewish community has come to be part of the Israeli civic consciousness. This, after an initial response of, at best, silent acknowledgment or, less benignly, straightforward denial or rejection. Differing accounts of the early "post-Holocaust" history within Israel continue to this day, and I do not propose here to judge those views. But there is little disagreement that in the period near and soon after the end of World War II the Yishuv's attitude toward the survivors of the Nazi genocide, as well as, albeit less openly, toward its victims, was even in its sympathetic manifestations ambivalent; in its more severe appearances, it was critical or antagonistic. After all, viewed at the level of ideology, the Nazi genocide provided evidence that the Zionist diagnosis of Jewish life in the Diaspora had been essentially correct: that that existence was precarious, dependent on the will and also on the whim of alien power, which could easily turn—and in "enlightened" Germany did turn—against it. Israeli Jews who regarded the Nazi genocide as cruel proof of the Zionist ideal were sometimes willing to say this in so many words; they were still more open in pointing out that European Jews had had ample warning of what might happen to them but had chosen to ignore it. Even outrage or sympathy or mourning itself, then, did not preclude a sense of the victims'—and still more pointedly, the survivors'—responsibility for their own fate. And then, too, more palpably, there were the survivors themselves: newcomers to a country in the making that desperately needed an increased Jewish population but hoped for additions different from the often traumatized and debilitated arrivals whose "going up" to Israel was motivated mainly by the fact that Israel was one country—for most of them, the only one—willing to receive them.

It is a long path, compressed into fifty years, from this early post-Holocaust response to the present—in which Yad Vashem, the national memorial for the Nazi genocide, serves also as the quasi-official symbol of the state, replacing the Western Wall (a religious symbol) as the site at which foreign dignitaries hosted by the state are expected to pay their respects; and the national Day of the Shoah (Destruction) and of Heroism, however strained this conjunction, brings a two-minute silence and standstill throughout the country. During negotiations for reparations with then West Germany in the early 1950s, and continuing to this day in efforts to compel a settlement against newly discovered profiteering by certain of the "neutral" powers in World War II, Israel has in a variety of expressions represented itself as the heir of Jewish victims of the genocide for whom nobody else could speak; at a lesser but symptomatic level, when plans for the U.S. Holocaust Memorial Museum in Washington were proposed, Israel objected that the appropriate site for such commemoration was in Israel, not in Washington or anyplace else in the United States nor, for that matter, anywhere else. Thus, out of ambivalent and wary beginnings, the Nazi genocide has come to be woven into the fabric of the Israeli national consciousness, both formally and informally, and the questions about this historical development now mingle with new questions about its future there, that is, questions about the extent to which this now significant element of Israeli collective memory can or should be sustained. The "future of the Holocaust" is an issue that confronts Jewish communities everywhere (as well as non-Jewish communities and institutions). But partly because other elements of the Israeli collective memory also have been challenged in the last decade and partly because of the complex and ideologically charged character of the Nazi genocide itself in respect to Israeli history, the issue has a distinctive urgency in Israel.

In addition to these quasi-historical questions, there remains a deeper metaphysical and religious issue that bears on the contours of Jewish identity in its most general terms. To write about the Nazi genocide from the perspective of a philosophy of Jewish history that finds in Israel the culmination of modern (or all) Jewish existence has almost invariably also been to judge the occurrence of the "Final Solution" as a warrant for the state—as proof of the need for the state and, correspondingly, also for the "ingathering" of all Jews to it; or as a reason, in this sense also a "redeeming" factor, for the state's coming into existence; or, at the very least, as a continuing "lesson" for Jews outside of Israel that attests to the contingency, or more strongly, the improbability, or *most* strongly, the impossibility, of a future for the Jewish Diaspora.

Admittedly, to live as a Jew in Israel does not require commitment to any or all of these principles. But to omit the Holocaust from a view of contemporary Jewish history or to regard it as indistinguishable from the broad spectrum of other moments in that history is prima facie implausible; the one practical and commonly held means of avoiding the latter criticism that does "omit" the Nazi genocide from its conception of Israeli Jewish identity does not incorporate a view of Jewish history at all. This is the nonideological claim of "native grounds"; that is, the cultural or psychological presumption (as well as the moral right, although this is a different matter) that having been born in a certain place is itself a prima facie justification for continuing to live there. For many Israeli Jews—no doubt for most citizens of most countries—the affirmation of their national or ethnic identity is surely rooted in this disposition. It is in effect a deflationary version of "post-Zionism"; it finds no place for the role of the Nazi genocide in that identity because it does not look for authority to any elements of Jewish history before or outside the state. This "commitment," like other autobiographical claims or expressions of feeling, can hardly be disputed, although the question of what actions it entails or justifies surely can be. It is in any event the other, principled or theoretical—and always historical—implications of the relation between the Nazi genocide and Israel that look quite different depending on whether they are viewed internally or externally; they also pose what seems to me a decisive problem for those who admit the relation at all.

For to take seriously the viability of Jewish communal existence outside Israel entails the *denial* of the three principles cited above: the Nazi genocide as evidence of the necessity of the state of Israel (and thus of the ingathering or immigration of Jews there), the moral-theological inference that sees in the causal connection between the genocide and the creation of the state a redemptive feature; the continuing practical and negative "lesson" taught by the Nazi genocide against those who believe in what then becomes the "illusion" of Jewish (i.e., minority) viability in an alien (i.e., majority) world. Nobody who attaches any of these conclusions to the place ascribed to the Nazi genocide in a philosophy of Jewish history could with logical or moral consistency commit himself or others to sustaining the continuity of Jewish life outside of Israel. Conversely, anyone who accepts the latter commitment seems committed to rejecting the inferred conclusions cited. At issue in this set of differences, and so for Jews everywhere—inside and outside Israel, although again differently for each—is the matter of place: of origins, but still more relevantly, of aspiration, of where and how they choose to live their lives and then the reasons they give themselves or others for doing so. This does not mean that there are not other grounds for claiming an important place for Israel in contemporary or future Jewish life outside Israel; still less is it meant to deny that there was a causal relation between the Holocaust and the creation in 1948 of the new state. (Almost certainly that relation was neither necessary nor sufficient, but then few historical causes are.) I would argue for both these claims. But both of them are quite different from the three metahistorical conclusions referred to, which see in the Holocaust proof at once of the necessity of Israel and the impossibility of Jewish existence outside it.

Thus, it emerges, not as an assumption but as the conclusion of an argument, that differences in readers' conception of their self-identity, extending to metaphysics and religion as well as to political theory, also affect the shape (and the reading) of the text presented here, which focuses on the elements—act and idea—of the single historical event of the Nazi genocide. Not only because that division would have consequences for any text that took the relation between Jewish historical and moral identity seriously but also because of the specific nature and historical character of the Nazi genocide itself. Readers of *Act and Idea* may well disagree, on a variety of grounds, with my assessment of the differences that shape their responses as readers; but they cannot, it seems to me, escape the existence of those differences or, after that, ignore the consequences of those differences for their understanding of what the Nazi genocide was. The position I thus urge for viewing the Nazi genocide in the context of a philosophy of Jewish history in which Jewish communities both inside and outside Israel have a continuing share—the interdependence of a single larger community—reflects a commitment that goes beyond any formal rules of justification. Some Israeli readers will almost certainly contest this view, as they may object to other, related or unrelated claims that appear in the book. But the issues at stake concerning Jewish identity and history are and will remain significant quite apart from the particular analysis presented here—even, or perhaps especially, in the shadow of the Nazi genocide. In this way, also fundamental differences may disclose a yet common ground.

8 | The Post-Holocaust vs. the Postmodern

Evil Inside and Outside History

The group that assembled to study postmodernity at the University of Virginia chose as its specific title for 1997–98 "The Question of Evil." My first reaction on being invited to address the group on the conjunction of those two topics was puzzlement. Surely, I thought, a typographical error had crept into this plain and sober formulation. "*The Question* of Evil"? Isn't a pair of scare quotes missing—that all-purpose defense against the menace of referentiality that would hedge those two words, or at least the too definite article, and so blunt the severe implication that there is only one such question? And then, also, what are we to say about the supposed object of "the Question"? For evil is as antique an item as any in the well-stocked museums of ideology, a relic freighted with moralistic lumber carved biblically from that one-of-a-species Tree of the Knowledge of Good and Evil. If postmodernity could be expected to leave anything behind, would it not be just the nostalgia for the binary or dualistic thinking that here opposes virtue to vice and then asserts that we can, and so of course ought to, tell—and retell—the difference between them?

Or perhaps, again, the slip might have been slighter, but also subtler and more inclusive—this, in the omission of a question mark at the end of the title, which would have posed "The Question of Evil" as a question itself ("The Question of Evil?"), in this way invoking the same reflexivity that postmodernity typically demands of others. Or then, turning to the other title in the conjunction, we might well ask about the odd nuance of the term *postmodernity* itself as it consciously displaces the more common *postmodernism*. The difference appears to be between the contingency of postmodernism—implying, like any *ism*, agency, the freedom to join up or to resign (as in socialism or Buddhism or impressionism)—and the fixity of the other, that is, the condition indicated by the *-ity* ending, which, notwithstanding the postmodern suspicion of facts without tears, denotes just such facts (as in *mortality*, for example, or, for that matter, *fixity*). And is it indeed the case that postmodernity is the "condition" we are in, whether we like it or not?

Puzzling as these reflections were, however, I caught myself before going further, reminded that, after all, typography is not destiny, that what appear to be lapses often turn out to have reasons (whether good or bad) behind them, that according to the most basic rule of interpretation we ought first to suppose that there was intention or deliberation in this title too, and that only if these remedies proved ineffective should any moves in other directions be invited. The same cautionary spirit suggested, furthermore, that we look at the "Question of Evil" as postmodernity itself first looked at it, in contrast to reading backward to it through the baroque superstructure more recently built on it; that is, that we consider "the Question" as postmodernity found it before going postmodern, in this way also learning why it decided on that career in the first place.

The framework to be proposed here, then, is in part a reconstruction, close to a genealogy, of the moral inclination or direction of postmodernity. Obviously, even with our own proximity to postmodernity's divorce from modernity—it is difficult to say exactly when this occurred, but it can't be long past—the lineage remains conjectural, although no more, I should argue, than conceptual genealogies ever are and in any event no more than those of the categories "modernity" and "postmodernity" themselves. A view of them as historical will, in any event, level the playing field, if it does not make it quite transparent.

Nor is the issue at stake a history of the development from one to the other as that "actually" occurred, since I shall be attempting only to place them against a common background of moral history, or more specifically, the—at least, *a*—history of evil.[1]

It seems clear that any attempt to describe a connection between these several factors from the vantage point of the present must sooner or later address the event of the Holocaust, or so consciously avoid it as also to address it: that extraordinary design for genocide that, whether or not it is unique, whether or not, more moderately, it was unprecedented, occludes the view, certainly the progress, of twentieth-century history and, more generally, of any moral (and so also, immoral) history that does not simply avoid this century altogether. For Jean-Françoise Lyotard, the Holocaust defines the break between modernity and postmodernity as a moral chasm marking the end of one and the beginning—less tendentiously, the onset—of the other.[2] This is a dramatic view of the role of the Holocaust within history in general, perhaps as far as one can take it without placing the Holocaust outside history altogether. And it is indeed to stress this limitation—the place of the Holocaust *within* history—that the present discussion is directed.

I mean to argue, in other words, that notwithstanding—or more precisely, because of—its moral enormity, the Holocaust is nonetheless to be registered and understood in empirical and historical terms. In such terms it appears as distinct, on the one hand, from metaphysical or theological or any other "transcendent" categories; on the other hand, from the bottomless ambiguities and sequence of ironies by which postmodernist ethics—the phrase itself seems an oxymoron—has typically fettered itself. The approach here considers first what stands on the two sides of the Holocaust, that is, of the line that marks off the post-Holocaust from the pre-Holocaust as it roughly parallels the related distinction between modernity and postmodernity, and as

1. For a fuller account of the concept of the history of evil, see Berel Lang, *The Future of the Holocaust: Between History and Memory* (Ithaca: Cornell Univ. Press, 1999), chs. 1–3.

2. See Jean-Françoise Lyotard, *Heidegger and "the jews,"* trans. Andreas Michel and Mark S. Roberts (Minneapolis: Univ. of Minnesota Press, 1990).

142

both those historical "moments" can be viewed in a non-extramoral sense, that is, morally. My thesis is that far from marking a rupture of or within history, the Holocaust is open to—indeed demands—historical, and so also morally historical, analysis and understanding. In other words, it must be placed in a historical field that joins its pre-Holocaust antecedents to the post-Holocaust aftermath. Indeed, the Holocaust as an event provides notable evidence for the claim of this continuum, which can thus also be read as a moral history or, less benignly, in a phrase I have introduced elsewhere, as part of a "history of evil." Certain evidence for this claim (as in an example cited below from Primo Levi) takes an unexpectedly commonplace form, although this *alltäglich* quality itself, I hope to show, adds weight to the argument for a moral continuum within, not outside, history and so opposes the claim for the end of one history and the beginning of another. In contrast to assorted apocalyptic views that claim that true history begins only when our own nominal history ends—here postmodernity shows vestiges of its modernist predecessors like Marx—the history of evil offers no hope of reprise or redemption. We find ourselves now *in* that history, as we have also inhabited it, although with a difference, in the past. According to this view, the intensity added by the Holocaust itself serves as evidence for continuity rather than for rupture, disputing also the diluted version of the "irreversible" break that Jürgen Habermas finds there as he strives mightily to sustain the pre-postmodernity project, that is, the ideals of the Enlightenment.

To view the traditional question of evil in its original terms is also, I believe, to invite the conclusion just stated, however one otherwise judges the premises of that question. For the question in its classical context asks quite simply how evil is possible—that is, given the divinely or morally ordered world in which it supposedly occurs—and yields the (also simple) answer that evil is *not* possible. Just as there are different versions of "the Question," so also there have been variations on this response, but their common core is clear: that however one otherwise analyzes or depicts the Holocaust, in the end, for the "Question of Evil," even that extraordinary moral enormity makes no difference.

This possibly startling conclusion follows for one or both of two reasons. First, the Holocaust makes no difference for the "Question of

The Post-Holocaust vs. the Postmodern

Evil" because that question in its traditional setting does not depend at all on the size or scope of the evil involved, its duration, or the extent of its consequences. When we recall Dostoyevsky's challenge to God's justice on the basis of the single tear of an innocent child, we confront the large issue of theodicy in brief: why, if everything happens for the best, should that single tear be shed? And for this question, the addition of millions of tears (or millions of lives) alters nothing. Without a justification for the one, there can be none for the other; and by the same token, to find a ground for the one would also assure a basis for the other.

The second reason why the Holocaust does not change anything significant in the traditional response to the "Question of Evil" is that given the premise of a morally ordered universe, evil has at most only relative or apparent force. All local occurrences (i.e., historical events) must be judged in the context of the whole. That whole, furthermore (by hypothesis) has justice or the Good or God on its side, which means in turn that taken all in all, it is better to have things the way they are than otherwise, with the implication that whatever is judged evil is only apparently so. In these terms, evil as such is also only apparent, at most a privation of reality (as the Platonic tradition has it), at its least a failing of human comprehension to grasp the totality of which man's limited comprehension is itself part. Human events thus occur on a cosmic and transcendent stage, with the wings of that stage spreading well beyond history. Evil is not actual or real; it is thus historical only as a "likely story" (in Plato's phrase), a variety of fiction and thus provisional, a station on the way to a larger truth, one part of a journey that only demonstrates its own insufficiency.

In reference to an event like the Holocaust the implausibility of this view seems egregious, but we cannot ignore the fact that it has the weight of significant traditions behind it. For the moment, however, its role here is to mark out one position on the map of moral history, which thus sets this one boundary at the denial of that history's possibility. The denial itself surfaces not only on a cosmic level, furthermore, but also in a related feature of the human domain. For a side eddy in the rejection of the notion of a history of evil also argues against the notion of human perfectibility, and thus against a moral history even in respect to human history alone. So, for example, the doctrine of original sin asserts the moral finitude of human nature; and the non-metaphorical point of that doctrine is constant and unforgiving even in its more moderate versions, as in the "evil impulse" described in the Hebrew Bible or through the concept of the body as the prison of the soul asserted in classical rationalism. According to these views, since there is no hope of escape from the limits cited, there is also little to say about the detail of their disclosure or, indeed, about any other incidents or acts in our common experience. What might otherwise constitute a moral history amounts here to only a recitation of episodes, a virtually random chronicle; any apparent pattern is no more than that of a constant present—proof of what is already known and what, under the aegis of eternity, has no significance. Thus, in the biblical account we find a reason for the creation of Eve after Adam but none, before that, for the creation of Adam himself. (Could what is omitted here have been the *first* bet God made with Satan, the precedent for what would then be repeated in the Book of Job?)

A second moment in the reconstruction of the history of post-modernity against the background of the Holocaust goes like this: Explanations of the Holocaust's occurrence have moved between two poles. At one of these—one that still draws on the first moment referred to above—the Holocaust is also (still) placed outside time and causality. In one such version it appears as a fit of national madness in an otherwise rational German history; in a second, quite different version it appears as an instance of divine retribution for failings on the part of the victims; in the majority of such accounts it is viewed as simply inexplicable or, in related tropes, as incomprehensible or ineffable. By contrast, at the opposite pole explanatory attempts replace transcendent with historical explanation. All these attempts include reference to the most obvious historical feature of the Holocaust's temporal and spatial location, namely, that it occurred, after all, in post-Enlightenment Europe, in the Europe of modernity, in one of the centers there of the high culture nourished by that humanist and liberal project. And the "Question of Evil" as it is in this way forced to be historical asks about that new setting in which it is found: Why and how is the connection between the two possible?

The Post-Holocaust vs. the Postmodern

This question itself, admittedly, faces a charge of circularity, as it juxtaposes two events and then asks how the juxtaposition is possible. But the writing of history is inevitably a matter of historians' lifting themselves (and their histories) up by their own bootstraps—the Hermeneutic Circle here bridging the past and the present—and there is, at any rate, no shortage of responses to the question itself. There is the evidence, for one thing, in the Enlightenment ideals of universality, addressed to pure and practical reason—that is, in both science and ethics—and positing also an essential and common human nature. These essentialist dispositions leave little room for any except the most superficial differences or particularity or individual commitments. Followed to their extreme, these principles yield conclusions that by now have become evident in the varieties of tyranny and totalitarianism that are all the more menacing in their exclusions or repression because they act in the name of truth. Admittedly, associating the Holocaust with such basic principles of modernity runs the danger of the *post hoc, ergo propter hoc* fallacy; it ignores the possibility, for example, that the Holocaust represented a reaction *against* the Modernity project (which would be a very different sense of *propter*), and there is no doubt that much of the Nazi rhetoric, at its manifest level, was directed against the Enlightenment's social principles of equality and liberty.

Notwithstanding these qualifications, the evidence seems to me compelling of the "filiation" of principles central to Enlightenment ideals and to the "emancipation" they heralded as those same principles later surface in practices of exclusion and domination; as the latter become embodied in nationalism and racism, they characterize the "totalitarian democracies" of which Jacob Talmon spoke[3] and leave signs of their presence even in the more liberal and nontotalitarian democracies. Theodor Adorno and Max Horkheimer's *Dialectic of Enlightenment* advances an extreme version of this view, but its central objection to the abstraction in Enlightenment claims of universality— the assumption that the universality asserted not only goes beyond all particulars but supersedes and dislodges them, in effect leaving them

3. Jacob Talmon, *The Origins of Totalitarian Democracy* (New York: Praeger, 1960).

no room at all—is compelling.[4] This is not, it should be clear, a claim of "No Enlightenment, No Holocaust," but few historical explanations ever purport to find necessary conditions for the events they explain.

Even a qualified version of this causal relation would provide a justification for the turn from modernity to postmodernity, with that turn then a reaction against the ideas dominant in the former. In this sense the Holocaust would indeed represent a rupture marking the end of modernity as justified in principle, with history and ethics for once acting in concert. And indeed, even if the syntax of "postmodernity" inscribes it as a "condition," in the way that I earlier suggested, its advocates have been much more involved in marshaling objections against the universalism of the past it claims to supersede than in considering its alleged accomplishments, such as the advance in moral history represented by the modernist discourse of universal human rights. But this discourse is by no means *tied* to the political or social principles that exclude or deny particularity, notwithstanding the *historical* link of that consequence to the Enlightenment. Thus, the search for an alternative might rest on this very ground, on the possibility of legitimizing differences among individuals or groups without precluding the possibility of transpersonal principles that hold notwithstanding the differences.

The danger in the postmodernist reaction against such universal principles is the familiar one of throwing the baby out with the bathwater. What I propose in contrast is thus meant, in relation to both the "Post-Holocaust" and the "postmodern," to save the difference between baby and bathwater and so also to save the one without the other. An alternative way of describing the need for this revision is to note that although the Enlightenment pitted itself against the obscurantism and superstition of religious or metaphysical thinking that imagined it could reach beyond history, it seems itself in the end to express the same impulse. For reason in the abstract, as Voltaire or Diderot or even

---

4. Theodor Adorno and Max Horkheimer, *Dialectic of Enlightenment*, trans. John Cumming (New York: Herder & Herder, 1972); see also Berel Lang, *Act and Idea in the Nazi Genocide* (Chicago: Univ. of Chicago Press, 1990), ch. 7.

Kant conceived of it, functions quite apart from any (and so also, it turns out, from every) instantiation. Only so can we understand the antipathy of these figures to parochialism or, in Kant's term from his essay "What Is Enlightenment?" to "tutelage" of any sort, even, presumably, if its consequences were uplifting or enlightening. In other words, the effort to displace whatever was claimed as transcendent turned out to produce another version of the same; like the other, it too was a- or even antihistorical. Scoffing at Pangloss's naive faith in this "best of all possible worlds," Voltaire himself espoused an optimism on behalf of the power of reason that is more like than different. Certainly it nourished in Voltaire, as much as it did in Pangloss (or Leibniz), an antagonism to particularity that in retrospect was at once ominous and prescient: I refer here, for example, to Voltaire's antisemitism and most immediately to his prescient warning in his *Philosophical Dictionary* of a "holocaust" for the Jews. In this way, the turn to modernity, which, after all, had anticipated postmodernity by reacting vigorously against the grand narratives of its past with their transcendent and universalizing impulses, fell victim to the same a- or antihistoricism of those accounts. In respect to their origins, the histories of modernity and postmodernity are very much alike—a fact that both have been eager to hide.

The difference between them, then, must be found not in their origins but in their futures, with the prospect for postmodernity at this point still open, poised between two main alternatives. The first of these would be to declare an end—well earned and well deserved—to modernity, marking a breach in history accentuated by the claim that in addition to the human agents responsible for the moral breach, the writing of history itself has also been at fault. For the same "totalizing" impulse that expressed itself through political action in the "total" state and then also in the Nazis' "Final Solution" would also express itself rhetorically in the total or grand narratives for which typically there was not simply *a* beginning, middle, and end but *the* beginning, middle, and end. The reaction against that principle then insists that for postmodernity, the units of discourse must be so small and discrete that they exclude—more strongly, give the lie to—any efforts to place them in a larger narrative, to view them as pieces of a whole. The purpose of this tactic is to break the lockstep of standard historical discourse without, however, losing the force of historical narrative. This option too, however, whatever its intentions to the contrary, seems to place certain events, together with everything under the heading of values, outside of history; certainly, in the absence of any pattern of relative connectives—causal, temporal, comparative—there would be no historical ground or order.

The alternative I propose here to the postmodern conception of a rupture in history is to view the evidence of history, the same history, as attesting to a kind of filiation or linkage between historical events, including even the Holocaust, in such a way as to allow (and then, of course, to compel) us to speak of a moral history as well as of a causal material history. Undoubtedly, certain historical events can be described apart from any reference to moral history, not only as an exercise in abstraction but because the latter is not especially relevant. (The Industrial Revolution might be a possible example of this, but even that only until one begins to fit it into the general framework of technology and man's relationship to nature.) And certainly the place of the Holocaust in moral history is as central *historically* to accounts of the Holocaust as any other of its aspects; indeed one can imagine that moral history without the others more readily than the converse.

The claim cannot be developed as fully here as it deserves, but I would begin that justification by repeating earlier assertions about the retroactive status of the Holocaust, that is, with the historian as moral agent, responsible for the account thus retrieved from the past, and with the representation of the past then part of a continuum and, in a perverse sense, of a progression. What I mean by this point can be stated in quasi-figurative terms. It would by now require a radical thought-experiment to conceive of a world from which the murder of individuals is absent, whether in fact or idea. Yet it is also evident that there would have been a point in human history when that was the case; we might think of this emblematically through the biblical account, as the interval between the expulsion from Eden and, subsequently, Cain's murder of Abel. Viewed thus, individual murder would, in Cain's hands, have the character of an invention, a new stage in the progress of evil (following the first, comparatively innocent transgressions of disobedience and then deception in the Garden).

In a similar sense, I mean to suggest, genocide marks a further stage in the same progression, designating the murder not of individuals but of the group qua group, including individuals, but including them through their identification with the group and then also (or rather, first) requiring the destruction of the group. Considered from this perspective, the concept of genocide not only designates individual historical events (like the Nazi genocide against the Jews) but also inscribes itself as a new element—no less indelible than the earlier ones—of social and moral consciousness. The features of this phenomenon, moreover, are recognizable only in relation to its historical place, that is, in respect to what is found or can be imagined on the two sides of the Holocaust: the difference between the pre-Holocaust and the post-Holocaust consciousness. (Whether the Holocaust was the first full instance of genocide has been debated, and I do not judge that question here; the crucial point in this context is that the Holocaust is an instance of genocide, and that it is also emblematic of that phenomenon.)

Viewed under the historical and moral category of genocide, the Holocaust thus expands moral consciousness by its power of invention or imagination (grotesque terms in that context, but there is no way of further reducing them); but more than this, reflection on the Holocaust also forces the viewer into history—in contrast to leaving him in the role of bystander, which is what "understanding" by itself would allow. One basis for this contention appears in the relation of language to the Holocaust, beginning with the term *genocide* itself, which we know emerged from the Holocaust, coined in 1944 by Rafael Lemkin most immediately in reaction to the Nazi's "Final Solution." Lemkin himself did not claim that the Nazi genocide was without precedent, but he did find that there was neither a vocabulary nor a codification of laws applicable to that occurrence. Thus the need for the term *genocide* in order to indicate its distinctive intention and consequences, as well as, in the realm of law, the U.N. Convention on Genocide of 1948, to which Lemkin subsequently contributed. The term and charge of genocide are so common in current discourse that it would be difficult to imagine a world from which they were absent. It is all the more pertinent, then, to recall how recently they have entered our consciousness and contributed to the shaping of moral history and, as I suggest, to a history of evil.

Another means by which moral history is embodied in the issue of Holocaust language is through an absence rather than a presence. This is the fact that even fifty years after the Nazi genocide no adequate term has yet been found or agreed upon for designating the people who were held and then almost invariably killed in the death or concentration camps. For the Nazis, these people were sometimes *Stücke* or *Figuren*—"pieces" or "figures"—terms typically reserved for things, inanimate objects; in more benign moments they were for the Nazis *Häftlinge*—"prisoners." When the camps were liberated, beginning in late 1944 and then in 1945, the headlines of the *New York Times* spoke about the "slaves" discovered in them who were still alive. But the first pair of these terms—*Stücke* and *Figuren*—are indictments of the speakers who use them. And the second and third of those mentioned are, more simply, false: *prisoner* implies a penal system of some sort, with procedures of judgment and punishment, at the very least of a prison intended to contain or keep the prisoner, and *slaves* implies that it was the labor these people provided that was a condition of their existence. But the people in the camps had neither of these behind or before them. Their "prison" was not meant to "keep" them, and they had no more rights within it than they had outside it, that is, none; nor were they even slaves, since it was at least as much their death as their labor that was expected of them. The people in the camps devised for themselves the term *Ka-Tzetnik*—from the initials *KZ* of the *Konzentrationslager*—and this is quite precise. But it also lacks a descriptive connotation that would place its reference in any more general moral or historical context. In respect to this concept, then, the search for language adequate to the Holocaust forces us to address history in the present, not only to observe or register the past. The inadequacy of language in relation to this or other terms bearing on the Holocaust might seem itself an argument for viewing the Holocaust as a rupture in history, the consequence of an event still beyond the reach of language. A likelier conclusion would hold that we are forced here to imagine and name the

The Post-Holocaust vs. the Postmodern

agents and elements in another stage of a historical progression that, although exceeding known terms and concepts, gains in intensity from just those terms, that is, through the detail—in this case, the menace—of history itself.

Much more would need to be said on theoretical grounds to elaborate the reasons for locating the Holocaust on a historical continuum that, with the addition of its own distinctive contribution, constitutes a history of evil. But this is, again, a continuum, not a broken line or rupture; a single history, not one that has been shattered and now has to start over again, beginning with its newest fragment. This point seems to me to be made clearly and graphically in what on the face of it is a commonplace episode recounted in Primo Levi's memoir of his year in Auschwitz. If it attests at once to continuity for Levi between the pre- and the post-Holocaust—and so also, as I would add, between modernity and postmodernity—it detracts nothing from the enormity of the Holocaust or from the challenge posed by that event to the standards of ethical conduct wherever they appear on that continuum.

In this part of his account Levi reports on an "interview" he had in the camp with a German chemist, Pannwitz, who was in a position to appoint Levi, also a chemist by training, to his laboratory and so to a job that would to some extent protect him from the worst conditions in the camp. At the conclusion of the interview, which, as things turned out, gained Levi the job and probably his life, Levi is led back to the camp by the Kapo, Alex, who had brought him to see Pannwitz and must now escort him back:

Alex enters the scene again. I am once more under his jurisdiction. . . . Here we are again on the steps. Alex flies down the stairs: he has leather shoes because he is not a Jew, he is as light on his feet as the devils of Malabolge. At the bottom he turns and looks at me sourly as I walk down hesitantly and noisily in my two enormous unpaired wooden shoes, clinging on to the rail like an old man. . . . To re-enter Bude, one has to cross a space cluttered with piles of crossbeams and metal frames. The steel cable of a crane cuts across the road, and Alex catches hold of it to climb over: *Donnerwetter*, he looks at his hand black with thick grease. In the meanwhile I have joined him. Without hatred and without sneering, Alex wipes his hand on my shoulder, both the palm and the back of the hand, to clean it; he would be amazed, the poor brute Alex, if someone told him that today, on the basis of this action I judge him and Pannwitz and the innumerable others like him, big and small, in Auschwitz and everywhere.[5]

Certain features of this incident are likely to elicit immediate assent in the reader. The most obvious of these is that compared with other goings-on in Auschwitz at the time, including other experiences recounted by Levi, this one is negligible, hardly worth mentioning. We hear about the swipe of a hand in a setting of gas chambers and crematoria. A second point, however, at angles if not counter to the first, is the ready recognition of what Levi finds wrongful in Alex's slight motion—not only wrongful but brutish and terrible, with all these terms extending farther than the fact that Alex had soiled Levi's camp uniform. Is it not reasonable to say that what speaks here, what sits in judgment—for us the readers as it did also, in the midst of Auschwitz, for Levi—is a post-Holocaust consciousness? One that for him, as writer, recalls the incident and reinscribes his initial reaction and that for us, now, ratifies that inscription? And can we not also conclude that however intense they were or are, neither of these reactions differs in its ground from what we recall or imagine as affective in pre-Holocaust moral consciousness as well? Far from marking a rupture in history, in other words, what is evident in Levi's reaction and now also in ours would be unintelligible if not for the linkage it assumes to ordinary (including pre-Holocaust) experience. Here too, it seems, a piece of modernity's moral stance, and premodernity's as well, imposes itself on postmodernity even as the latter speaks now with the voice and authority of Auschwitz. For the challenge in the Italian title of Levi's memoir, *Se questo e un uomo* (If this were a man), is just the challenge of moral judgment as such: the requirements and so also the contingencies that have to be met in order to be human.

In referring to this incident I obviously do not intend to equate genocide with the swipe of a hand; the association here points only at a common foundation that Levi himself suggests. Nor is the reference

5. Primo Levi, *Survival in Auschwitz*, trans. Stuart Woolf (New York: Collier Books, 1959), 78.

to such a small-scale event intended to revive conservative or reactionary skeletons that depend on such wisdom as "the more things change, the more they stay the same" or Ecclesiastes' weary claim that "there is nothing new under the sun." It assumes only an immediate recognition and assent to Levi's own reaction first to the initial event and then in his retelling it, and then an understanding of this commonality through what appears to be the one principle underlying it; namely, that whether we confront the episode pre- or post-Holocaust, pre- or postmodern, what is wrongful in it—and, before this, that it is wrongful—is evident: as evident, at least, as the quality of any human exchange or transaction can be.

Is the larger implication to be drawn from this small incident indeed the claim that nothing in moral history ever really changes, that we're condemned in moral conscience to a version of the eternal recurrence—although, as it happens, to a version of that cyclical view of history to which its most articulate advocate, Nietzsche, might have objected? Is it, in other words, no more than a revival of the old-time model of good and evil, now additionally burdened with all the standard "otherworldly" baggage? But I have already granted—more than that, claimed to show—that moral history does have a purchase in fact no more doubtful or tenuous than other historical modalities and that the Holocaust figures largely in this history just because of the changes it has introduced. This emerges, however, only as we view that history historically, placing the Holocaust within history, not outside it, and finding it together there not only with modernity but also, however reluctant its appearance, with postmodernity. Why should postmodernity be rudely pushed into this position that it has worked so ardently to escape? In the first place, because the post-Holocaust has provided no basis, at least none that is not arbitrary or ad hoc, for claiming a split in history that might then point to postmodernity as a *novum;* and then, still more conclusively, because postmodernity does not offer any more compelling evidence or explanation of its own.

Does this mean that there could never be an end to this or to any of the many other histories whose obituaries have recently been so prominently announced? Consider only the notable "ends"—of ideology, of art, of politics, of science, of philosophy, of history itself.[6] Why not, then, at the extraordinary crux of the Holocaust, an end to moral history, and so too the beginning of something else, quite different? To be sure, the very profusion of such announcements, in concert as it were, rouses a certain suspicion: might this group of supposedly independent discoveries be evidence rather of a fashion, that is, of a *style* of postmodernity? And then, too, there is other pertinent and historical evidence about such claims, which, as it turns out, have been made time and time before. Hegel, for example, proclaimed the end of art almost two centuries before Danto, and the predictions of the demise of philosophy as such have been so common and frequent that Etienne Gilson would find space for a pun to fit the crime. So he considers the long line of philosophers who proclaimed the end of their history (invariably, of course, as a result of their own achievements): "Philosophy," he notes, "has repeatedly buried its undertakers."

Lines of demarcation of all sorts have a certain attraction, if only that of the taboo. This allure generally would be further heightened by the prospect of living transcendently, outside history, of positioning oneself beyond the particular history that is declared to be over. But in shrugging free of the past in this way we are also obliged to imagine what a future without it could be; this is much more difficult to do, although not necessarily because of any deficiency in the imagination. I think here once more of Nietzsche, undisputed as a herald of the postmodern, who, having himself left good and evil behind, having transvalued all values, nonetheless, on that fateful day in June 1889 that marked the beginning of what would then be his own eleven-year ending, when he saw a cab driver beating his horse, ran across the square in Turin and flung his arms around the horse's neck before then col-

---

6. On the prospect of such "ends," see, e.g., Daniel Bell, *The End of Ideology* (Glencoe, Ill.: Free Press, 1960); Arthur Danto, "The End of Art," in *The Death of Art*, ed. Berel Lang (New York: Haven, 1984); Andreas Schedler, *The End of Politics?* (New York: St. Martin's Press, 1997); John Horgan, *The End of Science* (Reading, Mass.: Addison-Wesley, 1996); Martin Heidegger, "The End of Philosophy and the Task of Thinking," in *Basic Writings*, trans. Joan Stambaugh (New York: Harper & Row, 1977); and Francis Fukuyama, *The End of History and the Last Man* (New York: Free Press, 1992).

lapsing. Was that act—is it—so difficult to understand as a response to brutality or cruelty? Do we, in order to understand this reaction, require new moral categories based on the displacements of postmodernity, which would then supersede those of modernity? Or can we not rather infer a certain continuity, a grasp by the past on the present that extends also, or at least, to ethical response and judgment, that links the two in terms of principle as well as of practice? Titles or rubrics are the least of the matter, but on these grounds, "*trans*modern" or "transmodernity" would seem to have at least as strong a claim as "postmodern" or "postmodernity."

156

Hoping to find consistency between the postmodern Nietzsche and the impulsive gesture of a broken but morally driven man, between the Levi of Auschwitz and the survivor dwelling on a memory of the swipe of a hand, we might prefer to conclude here that like politics, all ethics is local, *only* local—*alltäglich,* perhaps also *allmählich* (gradual). According to such a view, it is not principles, whether moral or historical, that would then be at issue, but only individual moments of decision and design: no grand narratives, only simple or partial and, in any event, small ones. Most advocates of postmodernity have indeed urged conclusions of this sort. But I do not think in fact that such conclusions can or ought to be the moral of the hopefully moral, or morally hopeful, story recounted here. For one thing, this inference runs into a straightforward problem of logic: how could one justify ruling out— a priori, as it must be—the possibility of general moral principles, however time-worn they (or we) are by the time they are considered? And still more pressing than this is the historical evidence that does indeed point to the existence of a moral history—that is, ethics within history, disclosing there a texture of continuous threads or filiations, a woof as well as a warp. There is no denying the constant temptation to think apocalyptically, to hope somehow to manage to jump out of one's skin. Either that or, at the other, antiapocalyptic extreme (no less apocalyptic), the lure of individualism, of the autonomous self (that is, body): the hope that we may someday, somehow, become all, and only, skin. History is at times disjointed, often even shattering. But sometimes, too, among the fragments by which it reveals itself, it also, despite itself, discloses continuity and what look like recurrences and constants.

Admittedly, even when these appear, they provide no explanations of their occurrence, and often the explanations then summoned from the outside have occasioned more and sharper reactions than the appearances themselves.

Perhaps then it is the desire for explanations of the moral continuum that is the problem, not the constant failure to find it and the new pangs of conscience that such failures then add. Why not, after all, start with what we know, at least with what we *act* as if we know? For finally in moral judgment, even for the role in that judgment of the moral imagination, it is in the end what we do that at once judges and is judged by us. As a conclusion, this modest proposal may not seem much of an advance for either postmodernity or the post-Holocaust. But then it may be salutary to recall, in the same deflationary spirit, that there is ample precedent for this too in the past—that the advances made before them were also piecemeal and small, also anticipated, and also begun in what had come before them. Post-Holocaust understanding, then, is in this sense pre-Holocaust understanding. Only more so.

9 | Art Worship and Its Images

Something more than a century ago, Dostoyevsky, who put little stock in the idea of a future, let alone in the future itself, nonetheless ventured a prediction: "Incredible as it may seem," he wrote, "the day will come when men will quarrel more fiercely about art than about God." Two points now seem worth noting about this prediction. The first is that Dostoyevsky himself felt a strain in making it. The same writer whose "Notes from the Underground," that premature postmodernist, would blithely suggest that two plus two *need* not make four—that five, for example, could do nicely—stands sobered at the prospect of a future in which art evokes more passion and intensity than God. The change would be radical, and for this reason too he anticipates the difficulty of convincing his readers: "incredible as it may seem." The second point is that a hundred years later Dostoyevsky's once daring leap seems less thought-provoking than yawn-provoking. Who would now quarrel with his bold prediction or, for that matter, think twice about the commonplace of art (high, low, middle) as a more constant human companion, a readier source and goal (alpha and omega) than almost anything else real or imagined—including God as one or the other? For surely it is to the sounds and colors, the images cut to human scale in the arts of representation, that we now look most purposefully or perhaps still more often just because they're there. At other times also, as occasions for criticism, but much more for the pleasure of it, to be moved or uplifted, for confirmation of solidarity or common cause, and also, so far as this holds at all, to adhere to or believe in. All the functions earlier served by the ritual and objects of worship, among them God himself.

Dostoyevsky's prediction has thus come true. At least so far as "discretionary" values go—like discretionary spending, what is left after biology has its pound of flesh—art and the aesthetic have made their way to center stage. Admittedly, as for all claims of cultural preeminence, this one is difficult to prove by specific measurements. And of course the existence of values isn't demonstrated by the fact that they are professed: in an aesthetic age, first-person statements would be only another medium of fiction. Perhaps then by adding up the resources spent on them? That is, emotion plus money plus . . . well, even just space and time. But these are not easily calculated either. And then, too, there's the problem of deciding what to include (or exclude) as art. Music, painting, poetry—certainly. But this would mean all kinds of each: Bach to Rap, the Sublime to the Supremes; also film, obviously, and the telly too (with the average daily watch now four or five hours). Also, then, the thickened air of advertising and the extensions of style— cars, clothes, furniture, hair. The impulse behind this expanse could only be the will of artists to put their marks on everything that moves. That is, to be as omnipresent as God once was.

This impression, however, is still anecdotal, vague, certainly not rooted in sufficient evidence to warrant equating art's presence with the authority once claimed for a deity. A more responsive basis, however, originates in art itself, through the formula reaching back to Plato of the distinction between form and content and the conjunction it then posits for art of an aesthetic element and something else, extra-aesthetic, that is nonetheless required in order to give the first something to stand on. Art's soul is in this way joined to a body, with each of them obliged to fit itself to the other. The nonaesthetic "matter" may be as weightless as an abstract idea, which must, however, then be translated into rhythms or figures of speech or shaped image; and then, for the nonaesthetic elements of moral inquiry or verdicts, ditto. It is not that the aesthetic in art accidentally picks up such extra-aesthetic weight but that art could not otherwise make its way at all—that is, could not live disembodied. ("We must not paint eyes," Plato almost sympathetically warns the artist, "so beautiful that they do not look like eyes at all.")

Thus at times art turns directly to brute matter—to the medium; to qualified matter—the grammar of art's languages or the genealogy of the artists; and then, still more rarified, to abstract matter, ethical principles or abstract ideas that, however repressed or denied (or disguised), keep rising to art's surface. The broad tradition that recognizes these extra-aesthetic elements locates them *in* art if not entirely *of* it, and art and the artist then are obliged constantly to find the means of enlisting them, of joining body to spirit. Predictably, writers on aesthetics have differed on the proportions of the two elements, but few have claimed to rule either one of them entirely out. For some writers (including Plato himself) the connection between the two is central, with the two elements then interdependent. "A fair speech," Plato proposes, "can be made in behalf of a false thesis—but the best speech will be made in behalf of a true one." Even thinkers intent on reducing the distinction to one of its two terms have in the end stopped short of that last repressive step; Kant's advance on formalism and Marx's reaction against it both finally make concessions to what then remains as the Other.

For the discussion here, however, what counts is not the variations on this balance but the constraints internal to art on which whatever balance there is depends: the requirement that content and form must accommodate each other, that neither of these is self-determining or autonomous. It is just this sense of limitation, native to art as art, that has increasingly been lost in the newly sophisticated and now most common view of art, what impels the allusion here to its idolatry. That is, to "art worship," a reverence for images as they reach not only beyond their own bodies but, with that as exemplary, beyond any limits whatever. In art this move to sublimation appears within and without. Within, as art is alleged to transcend the limits of the idea of a medium or other material base (there is to be nothing on which art cannot work its magic, no subject beyond its grasp, no quality, however mean or narrow, that it cannot transform). Viewed from the outside, the disembodiment of art extends this impression of self-creation; art appears here as independent of history, weightless, untouched by motive, cause, or purpose. Thus everything becomes grist for art's mill, including art itself—with the implication, odd as this must sound in the community of idols, that no other gods can make this claim. At least not as well. Anything you can do, in other words, art can do better. More to the point, art can do anything you can imagine. In addition to what you can't imagine.

We have been lulled into forgetting that this view is recent in the history of art and aesthetic theory—an extension of the romantic conception of the artist as God-like in genius, giving the "rule to nature" (Kant's words) rather than the other, more usual and human-sized way round. That such piety rules in a time that views itself as skeptical, self-conscious, and ironic has not seemed to matter; a basic thesis of romantic irony, after all, was that the grasp no less than the reach of art is infinite, with the true subject of art being art itself. And since each previous moment in art's history also had art as its subject, whatever elevates art is itself also art; that relationship continues all the way down—except, of course, that there is no down. Thus we readily understand the intriguing exchange reported by Valery, as the painter Degas complained to the poet Mallarmé about his own frustrated attempts to write poetry. "This craft of yours," Degas objected, "is hellish. I can't manage to do with it what I want, and yet I am full of ideas." Mallarmé offers cold comfort: "It's not with ideas, my dear Degas, that one makes poetry. It is with words."

And so, of course, because words—or brushstrokes or musical notes—are themselves artifacts, there can be no constraint on their beginnings or ends; those too are part of art's process. Thus, the extraordinary powers now assumed for art of reflexivity and self-creation, weightlessness for both producer and consumer, answering—like only the most powerful deity—to nobody. Internally, perhaps, art may still be conceded a history: the moment of its actual appearance has somehow to be admitted. Externally, however, it remains ahistorical, first as an art-particular transcending its immediate circumstances and then later as it takes refuge in the genre of art as a whole. One does not have to go all the way with Derrida's insistence that "there is nothing outside the text" to understand that *inside* the text it is the words themselves—not history, not ideology, not even biology—that rule.

To be sure, other efforts have opposed this expansionist design. Two can be mentioned that lead to a reconciliation if not quite a synthesis of the conflicting impulses. The first of these comes from outside art, as a competitor in the battle of idols. For wherever places are disputed in the modern pantheon, science—notwithstanding its professions of skepticism, its constant willingness to find its own past obsolete—continues to present itself over all others, so self-assured in this that its view of art, when it has bothered to look at all, has been not so much antagonistic as patronizing. Nobody, science points the loud reminder, depends on art to send rockets into space or to cure disease. Measured by that standard, the limitations of art are obvious: it is decorative, ornamental, a happy diversion, at most a mechanism for survival. But not, in any event, a serious address to the "real" world.

But art quickly deflates this exaggerated claim with one of its own ready-mades: the evidence left over after science has done all it can—which still leaves almost undiminished the grist for art's mill, that human comedy where art's projects invariably begin. This is, admittedly, less than an argument; the questions of what progress ever accomplishes, where or how it advances, and what value it has—all these remain. Even if art in this setting claims a Socratic victory, boasting that art at least knows that it does not know (or progress), this means no more, finally, than that art cannot be outdone by invidious comparisons, not that it cannot be outdone. We see here in fact only that once idols appear at all, they become fruitful and multiply—notwithstanding the diminution this produces in their own standing.

The second, more directly pertinent evidence of art's unnatural status as idol comes from the history of art itself, in the Hegelian thesis not long ago revived by Arthur Danto, as "The End of Art."[1] For at the

---

1. Arthur Danto, "The End of Art," in *The Death of Art*, ed. Berel Lang (New York: Haven, 1984), and *After the End of Art: Contemporary Art and the Role of History* (Princeton: Princeton Univ. Press, 1997).

center of this thesis is the claim that art, like the genres within it, is as a whole a historical phenomenon, causally contingent—having once come into existence and so also with the prospect of passing away. Indeed, for both Hegel and, 170 years later, Danto art *has* passed away, displaced by the movement of mind or consciousness that (with differences in this part of their accounts) has since "progressed" to other projects. It is not, however, the claim of that actual end but the assertion in these accounts of art's contingency that shows, through the contrast it points, the idolatry—that is, the assumed immortality—of art that is being rejected. Here, in the contention that art does not determine its own beginning or end, does not create itself, that it acts not as pure spirit, not even as pure aesthetic spirit, limitations are acknowledged that bring into question the potency of this, or indeed any, idol. Think only of the midrash that gave a voice to the biblical Abraham as he destroyed his father's idols: "They have ears and they hear not; they have eyes and they see not." What charge could have more seriously harmed the image of these images?

The claim of the end of art, then, confronts art with its own mortality, as historically bound—an item of self-knowledge that must be salutary for the artist and his audience as well as for the artwork itself. More than this, however, it reinscribes a version of the question first posed internally by the distinction between form and content: What fits with what? That question now leads naturally to the question, What doesn't fit with what? and then to the question that becomes a constant refrain once we've noticed that art has feet of clay (or, for that matter, feet at all): Exactly what is it that art cannot do?

In one sense, of course, any attempt to answer this question will immediately appear foolhardy. Insofar as the imagination shapes art, to predict that art is incapable of conceiving or representing a given subject requires us to imagine what we are at the same time asserting cannot be imagined. No easy matter. Yet we can indeed say something about such limits, can think them if not know them, enough in any event to fill in certain features of art's contingent, that is, its historical self. My own version of this view, in elaborating the fault in "art worship," compresses large premises in a small compass: first, that art as figurative, that is, as non- or antiliteral, imposes a trope or swerve on

Art Worship and Its Images

whatever, or wherever, it starts from; second, that this process of figuration is tied to the being and style of the artist, thus that figuration is intrinsically personal; and so also, finally, that what art supersedes in its initial (and literal) object or occasion by the figures it imposes is thus meant to be enlarged—heightened, deepened, often if not always "beautified," and in any event improved.

The decisive question concerning art's limits would then ask whether certain occasions of art—events, qualities, or relations—by their nature resist or conflict with this project that I have claimed is intrinsic to figuration. In other words, whether certain events or ideas or characteristics cannot or should not be enlisted in the spirit of art because they say more for themselves, in themselves, than any representation or image could. Or because to figure and personalize them, given their characters, turns out in fact to *mis*represent and so to diminish rather than to enlarge them. The features at risk here may be cognitive or moral in character, or both, a matter of physical size (so Aristotle's warning against introducing to mimesis a creature "a thousand miles long") or of moral diminution (an ethical analogue of Aristotle's law of noncontradiction). And the violation of both these rules appears, as I argue more fully in other chapters before this, in many—in principle if not in fact, in all—images or representations of the Holocaust. It is not only, as would be readily agreed, that many individual "Holocaust images" have given in to the temptations of sentimentality or cant or sensationalism but that the subject itself gives emphasis to those disproportions because of the intrinsically impersonal, collective, harshly systematic act of the genocide itself. In this way, the causal structure of the subject—what it *is,* after all—conflicts with the means intended to accommodate it. Individual features of that subject have in other contexts been the stuff of much, and much great, art: the knowledge of mortality, the pain of loss, the expanse of love, the will to memory. But the specific context of the Holocaust which moves the individual and personal narratives embodying these themes—the context without which they would remain motionless—is itself not individual or personal or, for that matter, human at all. This is why, as I have suggested earlier, the most effective artistic representations of the

Holocaust have either directly appropriated the rhetorical forms of history rather than those of art or, just as explicitly, assumed the event of the Holocaust as a historical given, appropriated from outside the realm of art to serve as a basis for the artistic response.

I offer this example, even in conclusion, as a still too brief application of a more general claim. Other examples of the challenge that non-aesthetic content—history, ethics—may make to artistic form could be cited that come to the same point. There are no literary dramas of madness, nor are there literary "productions" with nonhuman nature as their subjects—and for the same reason: the absence from both of them of anything approximating individual agency or freedom. The madness of Lear is always a *half*-madness, still governed by reason; "animal" fables or the few animal novels that have been written turn out at second look to be human ones in rough disguise.

The formal conclusion proposed here is in any event broader than these examples: that just as within art we require a convergence of its aesthetic and its non- or extra-aesthetic elements, with certain possibilities on each side minimized or even excluded by choices made on the other, so for art as a whole, that is, as a genre, some subjects may exceed or be at odds with its capacities, thus indicating the requirement of a different means. The irony of this conclusion—that it does no more than apply an aesthetic principle widely assumed *within* art to art as such—strengthens rather than undercuts it. Nothing more, accordingly, than poetic—or painterly or musical—justice. The assumption behind this principle should by now seem commonplace, since it claims only the historical contingency and formal limitation of art. This, on the demonstrable grounds of the possibility of misrepresentation, in which the view of a subject is distorted and so diminished because of inadequacies in the medium by which it has been represented, the "stuff" constituting its images.

The issue of the specifically moral limits of art—the intrinsic relationship between aesthetic and moral categories and thus of the warrant justifying an ethical verdict in "judging" art—is neither less contentious nor less serious. Consider, for example, a statement by the poet Joseph Brodsky in his acceptance speech for the Nobel prize:

Art Worship and Its Images

There is no doubt in my mind that, had we been choosing our leaders on the basis of their reading experience and not their political programs, there would be much less grief on earth. It seems to me that a potential master of our fates should be asked, first of all, not about how he imagines the course of his foreign policy, but about his attitude toward Stendhal, Dickens, Dostoyevsky. . . . I believe—not empirically, alas, but only theoretically—that for someone who has read a lot of Dickens, to shoot his like in the name of some idea is somewhat more problematic than for someone who has read no Dickens.

Even allowing for the backing and filling in these lines, Brodsky's thesis is plain: there is an inverse proportion between the presence of great literature and the act of murder. But is this true? Brodsky himself concedes that he does not know it "empirically," and surely this admission holds, and not only for him. As harsh and unexpected as the fact appears, it is impossible to deny that we know very little about the moral effects of an "aesthetic education" (or the lack of one)—and that what *is* known is at best equivocal. To claim the high ground for art through the supposed uplift of its consequences—a version, as it would then be, of God's beneficence—is to claim to know more than anyone does, and something that is as likely to be false as true. To turn one last time to the Holocaust in this discussion: it is not the absence or failure of aesthetic education in Nazi Germany, neither among its individual agents nor collectively, nationally, that can be held causally accountable, even in part, for that event. Quite the contrary: so far as any generalizations pertain to the causal analysis of that event, the role of the arts and the position of the artist in public life were not less but more advanced in Germany than in other European countries of the time. It is impossible to know what would have happened if the role of the arts had been much larger than it was. But even to raise that possibility is to make evident its incongruity, not only because of the complexity of the Nazi genocide but because of the unresolved, and perhaps unresolvable, relationship that this possibility assumes between the art world and the moral or civic character of a society and its members.

It may be objected that this second example sets up a straw man much like that of the invidious claims that I have suggested science at times has directed against art. And a similar response would then apply: that just as art does not pretend to compete with science on its ground, so art need not, *should* not, present itself as a rival of ethics. But in its role as idol, art has made just this claim, with Brodsky's statement a moderate version of many much stronger ones. And again, it is not necessary to prove the contradictory to this—that the aesthetic life, as Kierkegaard distinguished it, is at odds with the ethical—but only that the possibility of the contradictory cannot be, certainly has not been, excluded either empirically or conceptually. I think here of the offhand but convincing remark by Diderot's Rameau in *Rameau's Nephew*: "It may be that I have always lived with good musicians and bad people. Hence it has come about that my ear has become very sharp and my heart very deaf." Or Flaubert's still more pungent statement in one of his letters: "Perhaps in my case, it is the heart that is impotent." This distinction between the moral self and the body's (or art's) organs may not be intrinsic or necessary—but it is the opposite, triumphalist view of art as all-powerful, conquering through its imagination and sensibility, that ought to bear the principal burden of proof and that also, for the reasons that have been suggested, is open to doubt.

I realize that this characterization of art worship and its images, disputing the doctrine of art's omnipotence, may in the end seem to be only one more version of crypto-fundamentalism—an updating, perhaps, of Plato's silliness when he turned his back on the arts except for their use in the nursery, a lapse parodied in another, much later world in Henry Ford's no less puritanical offer to his customers of any color they wanted in their cars as long as it was black. But I do not believe that the obvious objections to aesthetic asceticism need also hold against the more specific criticism posed here. For what I have been criticizing in art's modernist turn—its aggrandizement, initially by others but which then reappears in art's own self-image—only takes art at its own word in the much longer part of its history. There it was precisely the limits of art, the recognition of a body attached to its spirit, that were expressed and celebrated. In any event, we ought constantly to remind ourselves that for all images—and so also now, by implication, for art—it is not the idols themselves that claim sanctity; their worshipers do this for them.

Art Worship and Its Images

Index

Library of Congress Cataloging-in-Publication Data

Lang, Berel.
Holocaust representation : art within the limits of history
and ethics / Berel Lang.
p.   cm.
Includes index.
ISBN 0-8018-6415-1 (acid-free paper)
1. Art, Jewish.   2. Holocaust, Jewish (1939–1945), in art.
I. Title.

N7417.6 .L36 2000
704.9′499405318—dc21   99-085757

CPSIA information can be obtained
at www.ICGtesting.com
Printed in the USA
FSOW02n1827220917
38988FS